MONOLINGUAL

# THE OXFORD
# Picture
# Dictionary

NORMA SHAPIRO AND JAYME ADELSON-GOLDSTEIN

Oxford University Press

Oxford University Press
198 Madison Avenue, New York, NY 10016 USA
Great Clarendon Street, Oxford OX2 6DP England

Oxford University Press is a department of the University
of Oxford. It furthers the University's objective of excellence in
research, scholarship, and education by publishing worldwide in

Oxford  New York

Auckland  Cape Town  Dar es Salaam  Hong Kong  Karachi
Kuala Lumpur  Madrid  Melbourne  Mexico City  Nairobi
New Delhi  Shanghai  Taipei  Toronto
With offices in

Argentina  Austria  Brazil  Chile  Czech Republic  France  Greece
Guatemala  Hungary  Italy  Japan  Poland  Portugal  Singapore
South Korea  Switzerland  Thailand  Turkey  Ukraine  Vietnam

OXFORD is a trademark of Oxford University Press.

ISBN-13: 978 0 19 470059 7 The Oxford Picture Dictionary
ISBN-10: 0 19 470059 3
ISBN-13: 978 0 19 474002 9 The Oxford Picture Dictionary
                                      with Self-test CD-ROM
ISBN-10: 0 19 474002 1

**Library of Congress Cataloging-in-Publication Data**

Shapiro, Norma.
      The Oxford picture dictionary: monolingual /
Norma Shapiro and Jayme Adelson-Goldstein
              p.         cm.
      Includes index.
      ISBN 0 19 470059 3 (pbk. : alk. paper)
      1. Picture dictionaries, English.      2. English,
language—Textbooks for foreign speakers.
      I. Adelson-Goldstein, Jayme.        II. Title.
PE1629.S52  1998                          97-21963
423'1—dc21                                CIP

**No unauthorized photocopying.**

Editorial Manager: Susan Lanzano
Art Director: Lynn Luchetti
Senior Editor: Eliza Jensen
Senior Designer: Susan P. Brorein
Production Editor: Klaus Jekeli
Art Buyer: Tracy A. Hammond
Pronunciation Editor: Sharon Goldstein
Cover design by Silver Editions

Printing (last digit): 10 9 8 7 6 5 4 3 2

Printed in Hong Kong.

*Illustrations by:* David Aikins, Doug Archer, Craig Attebery,
Garin Baker, Sally Bensusen, Eliot Bergman, Mark Bischel, Dan
Brown / Artworks NY, Roy Douglas Buchman, George Burgos /
Larry Dodge, Rob Burman, Carl Cassler, Mary Chandler, Robert
Crawford, Jim DeLapine, Judy Francis, Graphic Chart and Map
Co., Dale Gustafson, Biruta Akerbergs Hansen, Marcia
Hartsock, C.M.I., David Hildebrand, The Ivy League of Artists,
Inc. / Judy Degraffenreid, The Ivy League of Artists, Inc. / Tom
Powers, The Ivy League of Artists, Inc. / John Rice, Pam
Johnson, Ed Kurtzman, Narda Lebo, Scott A. MacNeill /
MACNEILL & MACINTOSH, Andy Lendway / Deborah Wolfe
Ltd., Jeffrey Mangiat, Suzanne Mogensen, Mohammad
Mansoor, Tom Newsom, Melodye Benson Rosales, Stacey
Schuett, Rob Schuster, James Seward, Larry Taugher, Bill
Thomson, Anna Veltfort, Nina Wallace, Wendy Wassink-
Ackison, Michael Wepplo, Don Wieland
Thanks to Mike Mikos for his preliminary architectural sketches
of several pieces.

*References*
Boyer, Paul S., Clifford E. Clark, Jr., Joseph F. Kett, Thomas L.
Purvis, Harvard Sitkoff, Nancy Woloch *The Enduring Vision: A
History of the American People*, Lexington, Massachusetts: D.C.
Heath and Co., 1990.

Grun, Bernard, *The Timetables of History: A Horizontal Linkage
of People and Events*, (based on Werner Stein's Kulturfahrplan)
New York: A Touchstone Book, Simon and Schuster, 1946,
1963, 1975, 1979.

*Statistical Abstract of the United States: 1996*, 116th Edition,
Washington, DC: US Bureau of the Census, 1996.

*The World Book Encyclopedia*, Chicago: World Book Inc., a
Scott Fetzer Co., 1988 Edition.

Toff, Nancy, Editor-in-Chief, *The People of North America*
(Series), New York: Chelsea House Publishers, Main Line Books,
1988.

Trager, James, *The People's Chronology, A Year-by-Year Record
of Human Events from Prehistory to the Present*, New York:
Henry Holt Reference Book, 1992.

# Acknowledgments

The publisher and authors would like to thank the following people for reviewing the manuscript and/or participating in focus groups as the book was being developed:

Ana Maria Aguilera, Lubie Alatriste, Ann Albarelli, Margaret Albers, Sherry Allen, Fiona Armstrong, Ted Auerbach, Steve Austen, Jean Barlow, Sally Bates, Sharon Batson, Myra Baum, Mary Beauparlant, Gretchen Bitterlin, Margrajean Bonilla, Mike Bostwick, Shirley Brod, Lihn Brown, Trish Brys-Overeem, Lynn Bundy, Chris Bunn, Carol Carvel, Leslie Crucil, Jill DeLa Llata, Robert Denheim, Joshua Denk, Kay Devonshire, Thomas Dougherty, Gudrun Draper, Sara Eisen, Lynda Elkins, Ed Ende, Michele Epstein, Beth Fatemi, Andra R. Fawcett, Alice Fiedler, Harriet Fisher, James Fitzgerald, Mary Fitzsimmons, Scott Ford, Barbara Gaines, Elizabeth Garcia Grenados, Maria T. Gerdes, Penny Giacalone, Elliott Glazer, Jill Gluck de la Llata, Javier Gomez, Pura Gonzales, Carole Goodman, Joyce Grabowski, Maggie Grennan, Joanie Griffin, Sally Hansen, Fotini Haritos, Alice Hartley, Fernando Herrera, Ann Hillborn, Mary Hopkins, Lori Howard, Leann Howard, Pamela Howard, Rebecca Hubner, Jan Jarrell, Vicki Johnson, Michele Kagan, Nanette Kafka, Gena Katsaros, Evelyn Kay, Greg Keech, Cliff Ker, Gwen Kerner-Mayer, Marilou Kessler, Patty King, Linda Kiperman, Joyce Klapp, Susan Knutson, Sandy Kobrine, Marinna Kolaitis, Donna Korol, Lorraine Krampe, Karen Kuser, Andrea Lang, Nancy Lebow, Tay Lesley, Gale Lichter, Sandie Linn, Rosario Lorenzano, Louise Louie, Cheryl Lucas, Ronna Magy, Juanita Maltese, Mary Marquardsen, Carmen Marques Rivera, Susan McDowell, Alma McGee, Jerry McLeroy, Kevin McLure, Joan Meier, Patsy Mills, Judy Montague, Vicki Moore, Eneida Morales, Glenn Nadelbach, Elizabeth Neblett, Kathleen Newton, Yvonne Nishio, Afra Nobay, Rosa Elena Ochoa, Jean Owensby, Jim Park, John Perkins, Jane Pers, Laura Peskin, Maria Pick, Percy Pleasant, Selma Porter, Kathy Quinones, Susan Ritter, Martha Robledo, Maureen Rooney, Jean Rose, David Ross, Julietta Ruppert, Lorraine Ruston, Susan Ryan, Frederico Salas, Leslie Salmon, Jim Sandifer, Linda Sasser, Lisa Schreiber, Mary Segovia, Abe Shames, Debra Shaw, Stephanie Shipp, Pat Singh, Mary Sklavos, Donna Stark, Claire Cocoran Stehling, Lynn Sweeden, Joy Tesh, Sue Thompson, Christine Tierney, Laura Topete, Carmen Villanueva, Laura Webber, Renée Weiss, Beth Winningham, Cindy Wislofsky, Judy Wood, Paula Yerman.

A special thanks to Marna Shulberg and the students of the Saticoy Branch of Van Nuys Community Adult School.

We would also like to thank the following individuals and organizations who provided their expertise:

Carl Abato, Alan Goldman, Dr. Larry Falk, Caroll Gray, Henry Haskell, Susan Haskell, Los Angeles Fire Department, Malcolm Loeb, Barbara Lozano, Lorne Dubin, United Farm Workers.

## Authors' Acknowledgments

Throughout our careers as English language teachers, we have found inspiration in many places—in the classroom with our remarkable students, at schools, conferences, and workshops with our fellow teachers, and with our colleagues at the ESL Teacher Institute. We are grateful to be part of this international community.

We would like to sincerely thank and acknowledge Eliza Jensen, the project's Senior Editor. Without Eliza, this book would not have been possible. Her indomitable spirit, commitment to clarity, and unwavering advocacy allowed us to realize the book we envisioned.

Creating this dictionary was a collaborative effort and it has been our privilege to work with an exceptionally talented group of individuals who, along with Eliza Jensen, make up the Oxford Picture Dictionary team. We deeply appreciate the contributions of the following people:

Lynn Luchetti, Art Director, whose aesthetic sense and sensibility guided the art direction of this book,

Susan Brorein, Senior Designer, who carefully considered the design of each and every page,

Klaus Jekeli, Production Editor, who pored over both manuscript and art to ensure consistency and accuracy, and

Tracy Hammond, Art Buyer, who skillfully managed thousands of pieces of art and reference material.

We also want to thank Susan Mazer, the talented artist who was by our side for the initial problem-solving and Mary Chandler who also lent her expertise to the project.

We have learned much working with Marjorie Fuchs, Lori Howard, and Renée Weiss, authors of the dictionary's ancillary materials. We thank them for their on-going contributions to the dictionary program.

We must make special mention of Susan Lanzano, Editorial Manager, whose invaluable advice, insights, and queries were an integral part of the writing process.

*This book is dedicated to my husband, Neil Reichline, who has encouraged me to take the road less traveled, and to my sons, Eli and Alex, who have allowed me to sit at their baseball games with my yellow notepad. —NS*

*This book is lovingly dedicated to my husband, Gary and my daughter, Emily Rose, both of whom hugged me tight and let me work into the night. —JAG*

# A Letter to the Teacher

*Welcome to The Oxford Picture Dictionary.*

This comprehensive vocabulary resource provides you and your students with over 3,700 words, each defined by engaging art and presented in a meaningful context. *The Oxford Picture Dictionary* enables your students to learn and use English in all aspects of their daily lives. The 140 key topics cover home and family, the workplace, the community, health care, and academic studies. The topics are organized into 12 thematic units that are based on the curriculum of beginning and low-intermediate level English language coursework. The word lists of the dictionary include both single word entries and verb phrases. Many of the prepositions and adjectives are presented in phrases as well, demonstrating the natural use of words in conjunction with one another.

*The Oxford Picture Dictionary* uses a variety of visual formats, each suited to the topic being represented. Where appropriate, word lists are categorized and pages are divided into sections, allowing you to focus your students' attention on one aspect of a topic at a time.

Within the word lists:

- nouns, adjectives, prepositions, and adverbs are numbered,

- verbs are bolded and identified by letters, and

- targeted prepositions and adjectives within phrases are bolded.

The dictionary includes a variety of exercises and self access tools that will guide your students towards accurate and fluent use of the new words.

- Exercises at the bottom of the pages provide vocabulary development through pattern practice, application of the new language to other topics, and personalization questions.

- An alphabetical index assists students in locating all words and topics in the dictionary.

- A phonetic listing for each word in the index and a pronunciation guide give students the key to accurate pronunciation.

- A verb index of all the verbs presented in the dictionary provides students with information on the present, past, and past participle forms of the verbs.

*The Oxford Picture Dictionary* is the core of *The Oxford Picture Dictionary Program* which includes a *Dictionary Cassette*, a *Teacher's Book* and its companion *Focused Listening Cassette, Beginning* and *Intermediate Workbooks, Classic Classroom Activities* (a photocopiable activity book), *Overhead Transparencies,* and *Read All About It 1* and *2*. Bilingual editions of *The Oxford Picture Dictionary* are available in Spanish, Chinese, Vietnamese, and many other languages.

## TEACHING THE VOCABULARY

Your students' needs and your own teaching philosophy will dictate how you use *The Oxford Picture Dictionary* with your students. The following general guidelines, however, may help you adapt the dictionary's pages to your particular course and students. (For topic-specific, step-by-step guidelines and activities for presenting and practicing the vocabulary on each dictionary page see the *Oxford Picture Dictionary Teacher's Book.*)

### Preview the topic

A good way to begin any lesson is to talk with students to determine what they already know about the topic. Some different ways to do this are:

- Ask general questions related to the topic;

- Have students brainstorm a list of words they know from the topic; or

- Ask questions about the picture(s) on the page.

### Present the vocabulary

Once you've discovered which words your students already know, you are ready to focus on presenting the words they need. Introducing 10–15 new words in a lesson allows students to really learn the new words. On pages where the word lists are longer, and students are unfamiliar with many of the words, you may wish to introduce the words by categories or sections, or simply choose the words you want in the lesson.

Here are four different presentation techniques. The techniques you choose will depend on the topic being studied and the level of your students.

- Say each new word and describe or define it within the context of the picture.

- Demonstrate verbs or verb sequences for the students, and have volunteers demonstrate the actions as you say them.

- Use Total Physical Response commands to build comprehension of the vocabulary: *Put the pencil on your book. Put it on your notebook. Put it on your desk.*

- Ask a series of questions to build comprehension and give students an opportunity to say the new words:

► Begin with *yes/no* questions. *Is #16 chalk?* (yes)

► Progress to *or* questions. *Is #16 chalk or a marker?* (chalk)

► Finally, ask *Wh* questions.

*What can I use to write on this paper?* (a marker/ Use a marker.)

## Check comprehension

Before moving on to the practice stage, it is helpful to be sure all students understand the target vocabulary. There are many different things you can do to check students' understanding. Here are two activities to try:

• Tell students to open their books and point to the items they hear you say. Call out target vocabulary at random as you walk around the room checking to see if students are pointing to the correct pictures.

• Make true/false statements about the target vocabulary. Have students hold up two fingers for true, three fingers for false. *You can write with a marker.* [two fingers] *You raise your notebook to talk to the teacher.* [three fingers]

Take a moment to review any words with which students are having difficulty before beginning the practice activities.

## Practice the vocabulary

Guided practice activities give your students an opportunity to use the new vocabulary in meaningful communication. The exercises at the bottom of the pages are one source of guided practice activities.

• **Talk about...** This activity gives students an opportunity to practice the target vocabulary through sentence substitutions with meaningful topics.

  e.g. **Talk about your feelings.**

    *I feel <u>happy</u> when I see my friends.*

• **Practice...** This activity gives students practice using the vocabulary within common conversational functions such as making introductions, ordering food, making requests, etc.

  e.g. **Practice asking for things in the dining room.**

    *Please pass <u>the platter</u>.*

    *May I have <u>the creamer</u>?*

    *Could I have <u>a fork</u>, please?*

• **Use the new language.** This activity asks students to brainstorm words within various categories, or may

ask them to apply what they have learned to another topic in the dictionary. For example, on *Colors*, page 12, students are asked to look at *Clothing I*, pages 64–65, and name the colors of the clothing they see.

• **Share your answers.** These questions provide students with an opportunity to expand their use of the target vocabulary in personalized discussion. Students can ask and answer these questions in whole class discussions, pair or group work, or they can write the answers as journal entries.

Further guided and communicative practice can be found in the *Oxford Picture Dictionary Teacher's Book* and in *Classic Classroom Activities*. The *Oxford Picture Dictionary Beginning* and *Intermediate Workbooks* and *Read All About It 1* and *2* provide your students with controlled and communicative reading and writing practice.

We encourage you to adapt the materials to suit the needs of your classes, and we welcome your comments and ideas. Write to us at:

Oxford University Press
ESL Department
198 Madison Avenue
New York, NY 10016

*Jayme Adelson-Goldstein*

*Norma Shapiro*

# A Letter to the Student

## Dear Student of English,

Welcome to *The Oxford Picture Dictionary.* The more than 3,700 words in this book will help you as you study English.

Each page in this dictionary teaches about a specific topic. The topics are grouped together in units. All pages in a unit have the same color and symbol. For example, each page in the Food unit has this symbol:

On each page you will see pictures and words. The pictures have numbers or letters that match the numbers or letters in the word lists. Verbs (action words) are identified by letters and all other words are identified by numbers.

### How to find words in this book

- Use the Table of Contents, pages vii– ix.
  Look up the general topic you want to learn about.

- Use the Index, pages 173–205.
  Look up individual words in alphabetical (A – Z) order.

- Go topic by topic.
  Look through the book until you find something that interests you.

### How to use the Index

When you look for a word in the index this is what you will see:

the word    the number (or letter) in the word list

apples [ăp**/**əlz] **50**–4

the pronunciation      the page number

If the word is on one of the maps, pages 122–125, you will find it in the Geographical Index on pages 206–208.

### How to use the Verb Guide

When you want to know the past form of a verb or its past participle form, look up the verb in the verb guide. The regular verbs and their spelling changes are listed on pages 170–171. The simple form, past form, and past participle form of irregular verbs are listed on page 172.

### Workbooks

There are two workbooks to help you practice the new words:
*The Oxford Picture Dictionary Beginning* and *Intermediate Workbooks.*

As authors and teachers we both know how difficult English can be (and we're native speakers!). When we wrote this book, we asked teachers and students from the U.S. and other countries for their help and ideas. We hope their ideas and ours will help you. Please write to us with your comments or questions at:

Oxford University Press
ESL Department
198 Madison Avenue
New York, NY 10016

We wish you success!

*Jayme Adelson-Goldstein*     *Norma Shapiro*

# Contents

## 1. Everyday Language

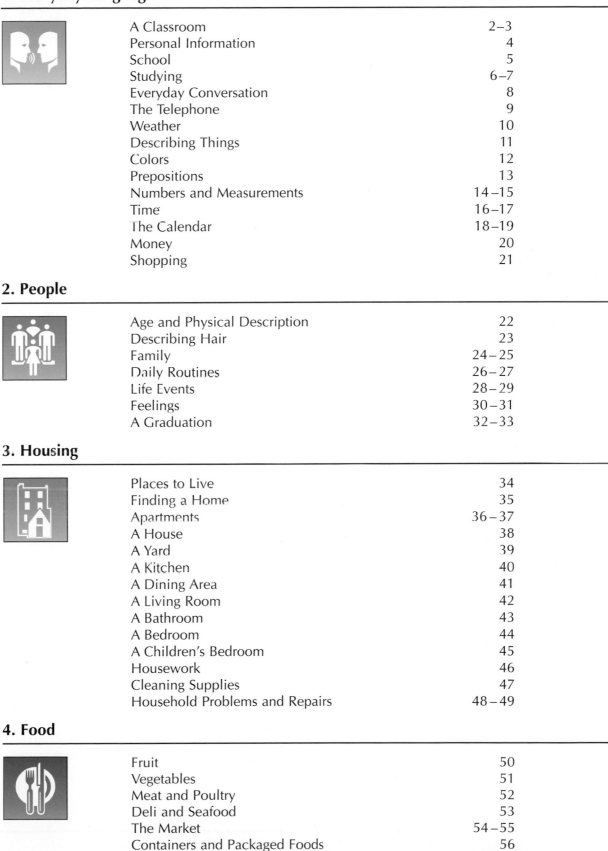

## 2. People

## 3. Housing

## 4. Food

# Contents

# Contents

**1.** chalkboard     **3.** student     **5.** teacher     **7.** chair/seat

**2.** screen     **4.** overhead projector     **6.** desk

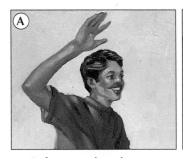

**A. Raise** your hand.

**B. Talk** to the teacher.

**C. Listen** to a cassette.

**D. Stand up**.

**E. Sit down./Take** a seat.

**F. Point** to the picture.

**G. Write** on the board.

**H. Erase** the board.

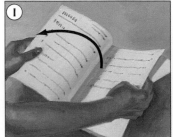

**I. Open** your book.

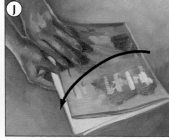

**J. Close** your book.

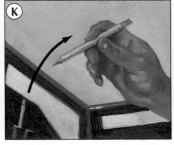

**K. Take out** your pencil.

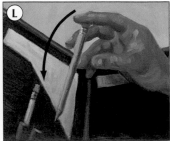

**L. Put away** your pencil.

| | | | |
|---|---|---|---|
| **8.** bookcase | **10.** clock | **12.** map | **14.** bulletin board |
| **9.** globe | **11.** cassette player | **13.** pencil sharpener | **15.** computer |

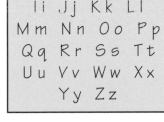

| | | | |
|---|---|---|---|
| **16.** chalk | **20.** pencil | **24.** binder/notebook | **28.** dictionary |
| **17.** chalkboard eraser | **21.** pencil eraser | **25.** notebook paper | **29.** picture dictionary |
| **18.** pen | **22.** textbook | **26.** spiral notebook | **30.** the alphabet |
| **19.** marker | **23.** workbook | **27.** ruler | **31.** numbers |

**Use the new language.**

1. Name three things you can open.
2. Name three things you can put away.
3. Name three things you can write with.

**Share your answers.**

1. Do you like to raise your hand?
2. Do you ever listen to cassettes in class?
3. Do you ever write on the board?

① SAM B. LARSON
② ③ ④

⑤ PINE AVE 446

⑥ 10

⑦ NEW YORK → Queens

⑧ NEW YORK

⑨ To: Sam B. Larson
446 Pine Ave.
Queens, N.Y.
→ 11364

(718) 555-6314
⑩ 2 ⑪
4 5 6
7 8 9
* 0 #

⑫

⑬ ⑭

⑮ SOCIAL SECURITY
911-00-0000
THIS NUMBER HAS BEEN ESTABLISHED FOR
SAM B. LARSON
Sam B. Larson
SIGNATURE

⑯ MAY 1972
S M T W T F S
1 2 3 4 5 6
7 8 9 10 11 (12) 13
14 15 16 17 18 19 20
21 22 23 24 25 26 27
28 29 30 31

⑰ CANADA
Ottawa ★

⑱ Sam B. Larson

---

## School Registration Form

**1.** name _____

    **2.** first name            **3.** middle initial            **4.** last name

**5.** address _____     **6.** apt. # * _____

**7.** city _____    **8.** state _____    **9.** ZIP code _____

   (      ) _____            _____ – __ – _____

**10.** area code    **11.** telephone number    **12.** sex: **13.** ☐ male     **15.** Social Security number

                                            **14.** ☐ female

**16.** date of birth _____     **17.** place of birth _____
          (month)  (date)  (year)

                                       **18.** signature _____

*\* apt. # = apartment number*

---

Ⓐ L-A-R-S-O-N

**A. Spell** your name.

Ⓑ B. 3. middle initial   7. city Queens
6. apt. # * 10
(718) 555-6314
10. area code   11. telephone number
15. Social Security number
17. place of birth
(date) (year)   18. signature

**B. Fill out** a form.

Ⓒ SAM B. LARSON

**C. Print** your name.

Ⓓ Sam B. Larson

**D. Sign** your name.

---

## Talk about yourself.

*My first name is <u>Sam</u>.*

*My last name is spelled <u>L-A-R-S-O-N</u>.*

*I come from <u>Ottawa</u>.*

## Share your answers.

**1.** Do you like your first name?

**2.** Is your last name from your mother? father? husband?

**3.** What is your middle name?

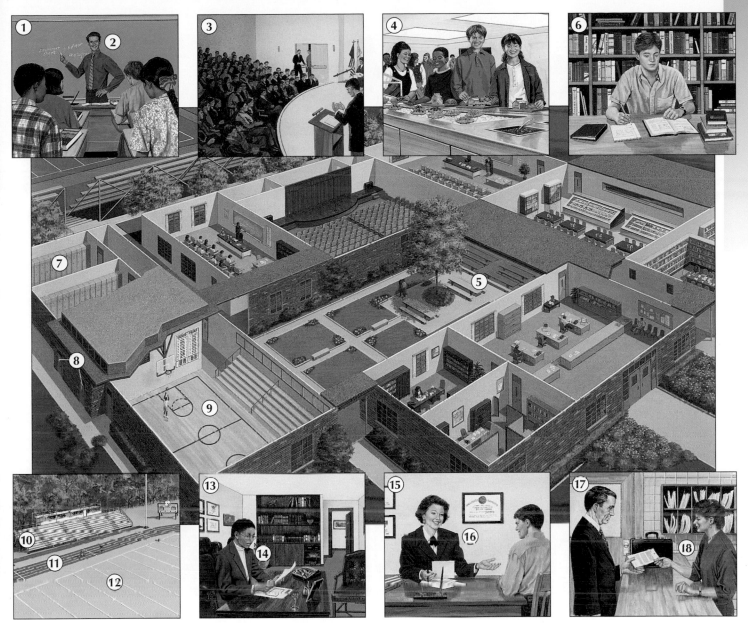

1. classroom
2. teacher
3. auditorium
4. cafeteria
5. lunch benches
6. library

7. lockers
8. rest rooms
9. gym
10. bleachers
11. track
12. field

13. principal's office
14. principal
15. counselor's office
16. counselor
17. main office
18. clerk

**More vocabulary**
**instructor:** teacher
**coach:** gym teacher
**administrator:** principal or other school supervisor

**Share your answers.**
1. Do you ever talk to the principal of your school?
2. Is there a place for you to eat at your school?
3. Does your school look the same as or different from the one in the picture?

## Dictionary work

**A. Look up** a word.

**B. Read** the word.

**C. Say** the word.

**D. Repeat** the word.

**E. Spell** the word.

**F. Copy** the word.

## Work with a partner

**G. Ask** a question.

**H. Answer** a question.

**I. Share** a book.

**J. Help** your partner.

## Work in a group

**K. Brainstorm** a list.

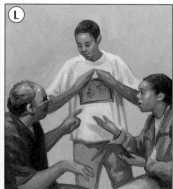

**L. Discuss** the list.

**M. Draw** a picture.

**N. Dictate** a sentence.

## Class work

**O. Pass out** the papers.

**P. Talk** with each other.

**Q. Collect** the papers.

## Follow directions

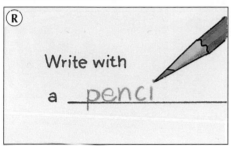

**R. Fill in** the blank.

**S. Circle** the answer.

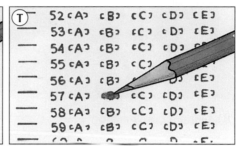

**T. Mark** the answer sheet.

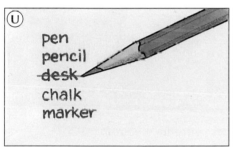

**U. Cross out** the word.

**V. Underline** the word.

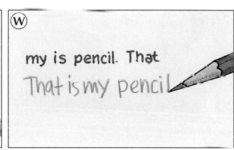

**W. Put** the words **in order.**

**X. Match** the items.

**Y. Check** your work.

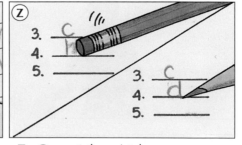

**Z. Correct** the mistake.

## Share your answers.

1. Do you like to work in groups?
2. Do you like to share books?
3. Do you like to answer questions?
4. Is it easy for you to talk with your classmates?
5. Do you always check your work?
6. Do you cross out your mistakes or erase them?

**A. greet** someone

**B. begin** a conversation          **C. end** the conversation

**D. introduce** yourself     **E. make sure** you **understand**     **F. introduce** your friend

**G. compliment** your friend    **H. thank** your friend      **I. apologize**

**Practice introductions.**

*Hi, I'm <u>Sam Jones</u> and this is my friend, <u>Pat Green</u>.*

*Nice to meet you. I'm <u>Tomas Garcia</u>.*

**Practice giving compliments.**

*That's a great <u>sweater</u>, <u>Tomas</u>.*

*Thanks <u>Pat</u>. I like your <u>shoes</u>.*

Look at **Clothing I,** pages **64–65** for more ideas.

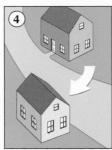

1. telephone/phone

2. receiver

3. cord

4. local call

5. long-distance call

6. international call

7. operator

8. directory assistance (411)

9. emergency service (911)

10. phone card

11. pay phone

12. cordless phone

13. cellular phone

14. answering machine

15. telephone book

16. pager

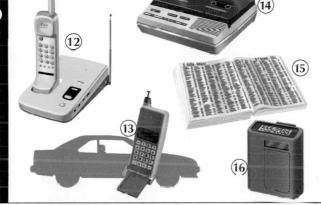

## Using a pay phone

A. **Pick up** the receiver.

B. **Listen** for the dial tone.

C. **Deposit** coins.

D. **Dial** the number.

E. **Leave** a message.

F. **Hang up** the receiver.

## More vocabulary

When you get a person or place that you didn't want to call, we say you have the **wrong number**.

## Share your answers.

1. What kinds of calls do you make?
2. How much does it cost to call your country?
3. Do you like to talk on the telephone?

**Temperature**

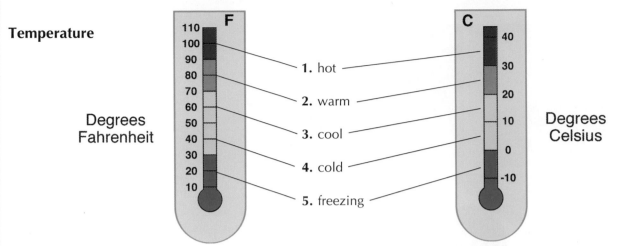

Degrees
Fahrenheit

Degrees
Celsius

1. hot
2. warm
3. cool
4. cold
5. freezing

6. sunny/clear      7. cloudy      8. raining      9. snowing

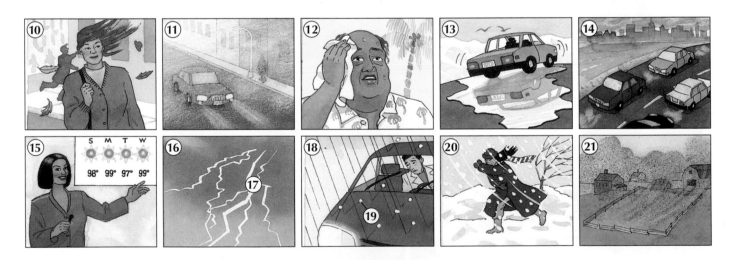

| | | | |
|---|---|---|---|
| 10. windy | 13. icy | 16. thunderstorm | 19. hail |
| 11. foggy | 14. smoggy | 17. lightning | 20. snowstorm |
| 12. humid | 15. heat wave | 18. hailstorm | 21. dust storm |

**Language note: *it is, there is***

For **1–14** we use,    *It's <u>cloudy</u>.*

For **15–21** we use,    *There's <u>a heat wave</u>.*
                         *There's <u>lightning</u>.*

**Talk about the weather.**

*Today it's <u>hot</u>. It's <u>98 degrees</u>.*
*Yesterday it was <u>warm</u>. It was <u>85 degrees</u>.*

1. **little** hand

2. **big** hand

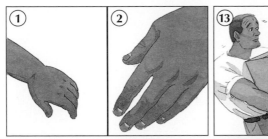

3. **fast** driver

4. **slow** driver

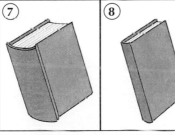

5. **hard** chair

6. **soft** chair

7. **thick** book/ **fat** book

8. **thin** book

9. **full** glass

10. **empty** glass

11. **noisy** children/ **loud** children

12. **quiet** children

13. **heavy** box

14. **light** box

15. **neat** closet

16. **messy** closet

17. **good** dog

18. **bad** dog

19. **expensive** ring

20. **cheap** ring

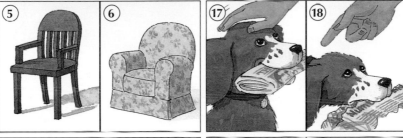

21. **beautiful** view

22. **ugly** view

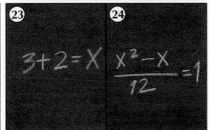

23. **easy** problem

24. **difficult** problem/ **hard** problem

---

**Use the new language.**

1. Name three things that are thick.

2. Name three things that are soft.

3. Name three things that are heavy.

**Share your answers.**

1. Are you a slow driver or a fast driver?

2. Do you have a neat closet or a messy closet?

3. Do you like loud or quiet parties?

| | | |
|---|---|---|
| **1.** blue | **6.** orange | **11.** brown |
| **2.** dark blue | **7.** purple | **12.** yellow |
| **3.** light blue | **8.** green | **13.** red |
| **4.** turquoise | **9.** beige | **14.** white |
| **5.** gray | **10.** pink | **15.** black |

**Use the new language.**
Look at **Clothing I,** pages **64–65.**
Name the colors of the clothing you see.
*That's a dark blue suit.*

**Share your answers.**
1. What colors are you wearing today?
2. What colors do you like?
3. Is there a color you don't like? What is it?

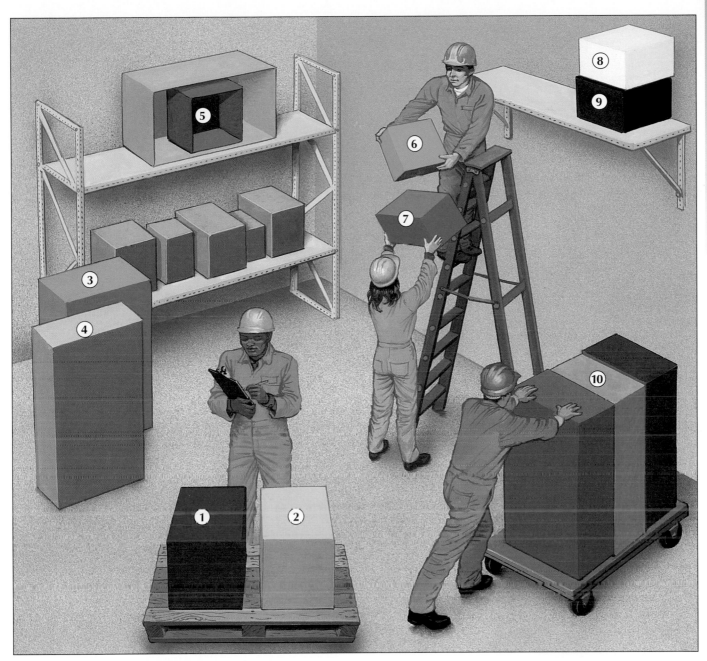

1. The red box is **next to** the yellow box, **on the left.**

2. The yellow box is **next to** the red box, **on the right.**

3. The turquoise box is **behind** the gray box.

4. The gray box is **in front of** the turquoise box.

5. The dark blue box is **in** the beige box.

6. The green box is **above** the orange box.

7. The orange box is **below** the green box.

8. The white box is **on** the black box.

9. The black box is **under** the white box.

10. The pink box is **between** the purple box and the brown box.

**More vocabulary**

**near:** in the same area
*The white box is **near** the black box.*

**far from:** not near
*The red box is **far from** the black box.*

13

# Numbers and Measurements

HOME **1** **8**
VISITOR **2** **2**

**SAN DIEGO**
**235 miles**

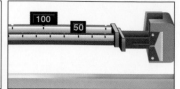

## Cardinals

| | | | |
|---|---|---|---|
| 0 zero | 11 eleven | 21 twenty-one | 101 |
| | | | one hundred one |
| 1 one | 12 twelve | 22 twenty-two | 1,000 |
| | | | one thousand |
| 2 two | 13 thirteen | 30 thirty | 1,001 |
| | | | one thousand one |
| 3 three | 14 fourteen | 40 forty | 10,000 |
| | | | ten thousand |
| 4 four | 15 fifteen | 50 fifty | 100,000 |
| | | | one hundred thousand |
| 5 five | 16 sixteen | 60 sixty | 1,000,000 |
| | | | one million |
| 6 six | 17 seventeen | 70 seventy | 1,000,000,000 |
| | | | one billion |
| 7 seven | 18 eighteen | 80 eighty | |
| 8 eight | 19 nineteen | 90 ninety | |
| 9 nine | 20 twenty | 100 one hundred | |
| 10 ten | | | |

## Ordinals

| | | |
|---|---|---|
| 1st first | 8th eighth | 15th fifteenth |
| 2nd second | 9th ninth | 16th sixteenth |
| 3rd third | 10th tenth | 17th seventeenth |
| 4th fourth | 11th eleventh | 18th eighteenth |
| 5th fifth | 12th twelfth | 19th nineteenth |
| 6th sixth | 13th thirteenth | 20th twentieth |
| 7th seventh | 14th fourteenth | |

## Roman numerals

| | | | | | |
|---|---|---|---|---|---|
| I | = 1 | VII | = 7 | XXX | = 30 |
| II | = 2 | VIII | = 8 | XL | = 40 |
| III | = 3 | IX | = 9 | L | = 50 |
| IV | = 4 | X | = 10 | C | = 100 |
| V | = 5 | XV | = 15 | D | = 500 |
| VI | = 6 | XX | = 20 | M | = 1,000 |

## Fractions

**1.** 1/8   one-eighth    **2.** 1/4   one-fourth    **3.** 1/3   one-third

**4.** 1/2   one-half    **5.** 3/4   three-fourths    **6.** 1   whole

## Percents

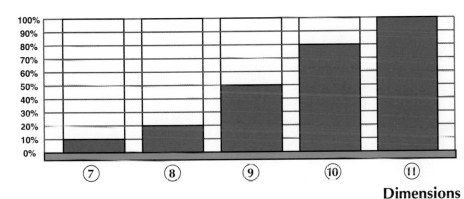

**7.** 10%     ten percent

**8.** 20%     twenty percent

**9.** 50%     fifty percent

**10.** 80%     eighty percent

**11.** 100%    one hundred percent

## Dimensions

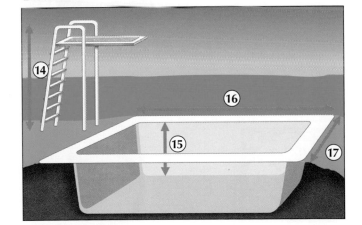

## Measurement

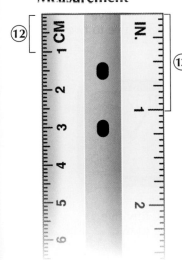

**12.** centimeter [cm]

**13.** inch [in.]

### Equivalencies

| | |
|---|---|
| 1 inch | = 2.54 centimeters |
| 1 yard | = .91 meters |
| 1 mile | = 1.6 kilometers |

| | |
|---|---|
| 12 inches | = 1 foot |
| 3 feet | = 1 yard |
| 1,760 yards | = 1 mile |

**14.** height

**15.** depth

**16.** length

**17.** width

## More vocabulary

**measure:** to find the size or amount of something

**count:** to find the total number of something

## Share your answers.

**1.** How many students are in class today?

**2.** Who was the first person in class today?

**3.** How far is it from your home to your school?

# Time

**1.** second

**2.** minute    **3.** hour

A.M.

P.M.

**4.** 1:00
one o'clock

**5.** 1:05
one-oh-five
five after one

**6.** 1:10
one-ten
ten after one

**7.** 1:15
one-fifteen
a quarter after one

**8.** 1:20
one-twenty
twenty after one

**9.** 1:25
one twenty-five
twenty-five after one

**10.** 1:30
one-thirty
half past one

**11.** 1:35
one thirty-five
twenty-five to two

**12.** 1:40
one-forty
twenty to two

**13.** 1:45
one forty-five
a quarter to two

**14.** 1:50
one-fifty
ten to two

**15.** 1:55
one fifty-five
five to two

**Talk about the time.**

*What time is it? It's <u>10:00 a.m.</u>*

*What time do you wake up on weekdays? At <u>6:30 a.m.</u>*

*What time do you wake up on weekends? At <u>9:30 a.m.</u>*

**Share your answers.**

1. How many hours a day do you study English?

2. You are meeting friends at 1:00. How long will you wait for them if they are late?

**16.** morning

**17.** noon

**18.** afternoon

**19.** evening

**20.** night

**21.** midnight

**22.** early

**23.** late

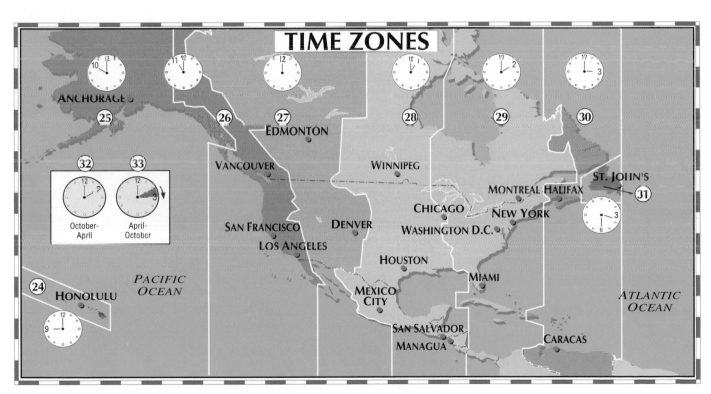

TIME ZONES

**24.** Hawaii-Aleutian time

**25.** Alaska time

**26.** Pacific time

**27.** mountain time

**28.** central time

**29.** eastern time

**30.** Atlantic time

**31.** Newfoundland time

**32.** standard time

**33.** daylight saving time

---

**More vocabulary**

**on time:** not early and not late

*He's **on time**.*

**Share your answers.**

1. When do you watch television? study? do housework?

2. Do you come to class on time? early? late?

**Days of the week**

1. Sunday

2. Monday

3. Tuesday

4. Wednesday

5. Thursday

6. Friday

7. Saturday

8. year

9. month

10. day

11. week

12. weekdays

13. weekend

14. date

15. today

16. tomorrow

17. yesterday

18. last week

19. this week

20. next week

21. every day

22. once a week

23. twice a week

24. three times a week

**2001** ⑧ ⑨ **❖JANUARY❖** **2001**

| ① SUN | ② MON | ③ TUE | ④ WED | ⑤ THU | ⑥ FRI | ⑦ SAT |
|---|---|---|---|---|---|---|
| | ⑩ 1 | 2 | 3 | 4 | 5 | 6 |
| 7 | 8 | 9 | 10 | 11 | 12 | 13 |
| 14 | 15 | 16 | ⑪ 17 | 18 | 19 | 20 |
| 21 | 22 | 23 | ⑫ 24 | 25 | 26 | ⑬ 27 |
| 28 | 29 | 30 | 31 | | | |

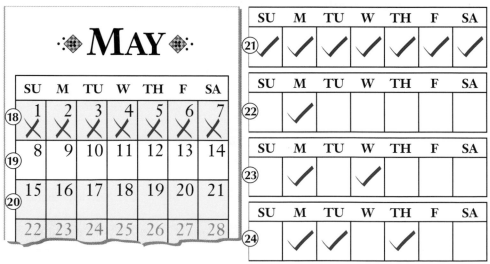

**❖ MAY ❖**

| SU | M | TU | W | TH | F | SA |
|---|---|---|---|---|---|---|
| ⑱ 1 | 2 | 3 | 4 | 5 | 6 | 7 |
| ⑲ 8 | 9 | 10 | 11 | 12 | 13 | 14 |
| ⑳ 15 | 16 | 17 | 18 | 19 | 20 | 21 |
| 22 | 23 | 24 | 25 | 26 | 27 | 28 |

---

**Talk about the calendar.**

*What's today's date? It's <u>March 10th</u>.*

*What day is it? It's <u>Tuesday</u>.*

*What day was yesterday? It was <u>Monday</u>.*

**Share your answers.**

1. How often do you come to school?

2. How long have you been in this school?

## 2001

### JAN (25)
| SUN | MON | TUE | WED | THU | FRI | SAT |
|---|---|---|---|---|---|---|
| | 1 | 2 | 3 | 4 | 5 | 6 |
| 7 | 8 | 9 | 10 | 11 | 12 | 13 |
| 14 | 15 | 16 | 17 | 18 | 19 | 20 |
| 21 | 22 | 23 | 24 | 25 | 26 | 27 |
| 28 | 29 | 30 | 31 | | | |

### FEB (26)
| SUN | MON | TUE | WED | THU | FRI | SAT |
|---|---|---|---|---|---|---|
| | | | | 1 | 2 | 3 |
| 4 | 5 | 6 | 7 | 8 | 9 | 10 |
| 11 | 12 | 13 | 14 | 15 | 16 | 17 |
| 18 | 19 | 20 | 21 | 22 | 23 | 24 |
| 25 | 26 | 27 | 28 | | | |

### MAR (27)
| SUN | MON | TUE | WED | THU | FRI | SAT |
|---|---|---|---|---|---|---|
| | | | | 1 | 2 | 3 |
| 4 | 5 | 6 | 7 | 8 | 9 | 10 |
| 11 | 12 | 13 | 14 | 15 | 16 | 17 |
| 18 | 19 | 20 | 21 | 22 | 23 | 24 |
| 25 | 26 | 27 | 28 | 29 | 30 | 31 |

### APR (28)
| SUN | MON | TUE | WED | THU | FRI | SAT |
|---|---|---|---|---|---|---|
| 1 | 2 | 3 | 4 | 5 | 6 | 7 |
| 8 | 9 | 10 | 11 | 12 | 13 | 14 |
| 15 | 16 | 17 | 18 | 19 | 20 | 21 |
| 22 | 23 | 24 | 25 | 26 | 27 | 28 |
| 29 | 30 | | | | | |

### MAY (29)
| SUN | MON | TUE | WED | THU | FRI | SAT |
|---|---|---|---|---|---|---|
| | | 1 | 2 | 3 | 4 | 5 |
| 6 | 7 | 8 | 9 | 10 | 11 | 12 |
| 13 | 14 | 15 | 16 | 17 | 18 | 19 |
| 20 | 21 | 22 | 23 | 24 | 25 | 26 |
| 27 | 28 | 29 | 30 | 31 | | |

### JUN (30)
| SUN | MON | TUE | WED | THU | FRI | SAT |
|---|---|---|---|---|---|---|
| | | | | | 1 | 2 |
| 3 | 4 | 5 | 6 | 7 | 8 | 9 |
| 10 | 11 | 12 | 13 | 14 | 15 | 16 |
| 17 | 18 | 19 | 20 | 21 | 22 | 23 |
| 24 | 25 | 26 | 27 | 28 | 29 | 30 |

### JUL (31)
| SUN | MON | TUE | WED | THU | FRI | SAT |
|---|---|---|---|---|---|---|
| 1 | 2 | 3 | 4 | 5 | 6 | 7 |
| 8 | 9 | 10 | 11 | 12 | 13 | 14 |
| 15 | 16 | 17 | 18 | 19 | 20 | 21 |
| 22 | 23 | 24 | 25 | 26 | 27 | 28 |
| 29 | 30 | 31 | | | | |

### AUG (32)
| SUN | MON | TUE | WED | THU | FRI | SAT |
|---|---|---|---|---|---|---|
| | | | 1 | 2 | 3 | 4 |
| 5 | 6 | 7 | 8 | 9 | 10 | 11 |
| 12 | 13 | 14 | 15 | 16 | 17 | 18 |
| 19 | 20 | 21 | 22 | 23 | 24 | 25 |
| 26 | 27 | 28 | 29 | 30 | 31 | |

### SEP (33)
| SUN | MON | TUE | WED | THU | FRI | SAT |
|---|---|---|---|---|---|---|
| | | | | | | 1 |
| 2 | 3 | 4 | 5 | 6 | 7 | 8 |
| 9 | 10 | 11 | 12 | 13 | 14 | 15 |
| 16 | 17 | 18 | 19 | 20 | 21 | 22 |
| 23/30 | 24 | 25 | 26 | 27 | 28 | 29 |

### OCT (34)
| SUN | MON | TUE | WED | THU | FRI | SAT |
|---|---|---|---|---|---|---|
| | 1 | 2 | 3 | 4 | 5 | 6 |
| 7 | 8 | 9 | 10 | 11 | 12 | 13 |
| 14 | 15 | 16 | 17 | 18 | 19 | 20 |
| 21 | 22 | 23 | 24 | 25 | 26 | 27 |
| 28 | 29 | 30 | 31 | | | |

### NOV (35)
| SUN | MON | TUE | WED | THU | FRI | SAT |
|---|---|---|---|---|---|---|
| | | | | 1 | 2 | 3 |
| 4 | 5 | 6 | 7 | 8 | 9 | 10 |
| 11 | 12 | 13 | 14 | 15 | 16 | 17 |
| 18 | 19 | 20 | 21 | 22 | 23 | 24 |
| 25 | 26 | 27 | 28 | 29 | 30 | |

### DEC (36)
| SUN | MON | TUE | WED | THU | FRI | SAT |
|---|---|---|---|---|---|---|
| | | | | | | 1 |
| 2 | 3 | 4 | 5 | 6 | 7 | 8 |
| 9 | 10 | 11 | 12 | 13 | 14 | 15 |
| 16 | 17 | 18 | 19 | 20 | 21 | 22 |
| 23/30 | 24/31 | 25 | 26 | 27 | 28 | 29 |

## Months of the year

**25.** January

**26.** February

**27.** March

**28.** April

**29.** May

**30.** June

**31.** July

**32.** August

**33.** September

**34.** October

**35.** November

**36.** December

## Seasons

**37.** spring

**38.** summer

**39.** fall

**40.** winter

**41.** birthday

**42.** anniversary

**43.** legal holiday

**44.** religious holiday

**45.** appointment

**46.** vacation

MARCH 21

JUNE 21

SEPT. 21

DEC. 21

(37)

(41) JUNE 5 — TIM!

(42) MARCH 2 — ANNIVERSARY

(43) JULY 4 — INDEPENDENCE DAY — STATE BANK — CLOSED - JULY 4

(44) APRIL 4 — EASTER SUNDAY

(45) MAY 17 — DOCTOR 4:30

(46) AUGUST

**Use the new language.**
Look at the **ordinal numbers** on page **14**.
Use ordinal numbers to say the date.
*It's June 5th. It's the fifth.*

**Talk about your birthday.**
*My birthday is in the winter.*
*My birthday is in January.*
*My birthday is on January twenty-sixth.*

# Money

## Coins

**1.** $.01 = 1¢
a penny/1 cent

**2.** $.05 = 5¢
a nickel/5 cents

**3.** $.10 = 10¢
a dime/10 cents

**4.** $.25 = 25¢
a quarter/25 cents

**5.** $.50 = 50¢
a half dollar

**6.** $1.00
a silver dollar

## Bills

**7.** $1.00
a dollar

**8.** $5.00
five dollars

**9.** $10.00
ten dollars

**10.** $20.00
twenty dollars

**11.** $50.00
fifty dollars

**12.** $100.00
one hundred dollars

## Ways to pay

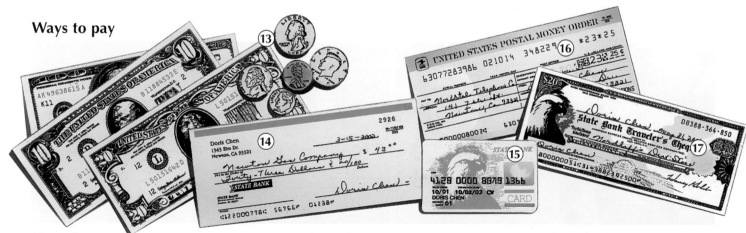

**13.** cash

**14.** personal check

**15.** credit card

**16.** money order

**17.** traveler's check

---

**More vocabulary**

**borrow:** to get money from someone and return it later

**lend:** to give money to someone and get it back later

**pay back:** to return the money that you borrowed

**Other ways to talk about money:**

a dollar bill or a one

a five-dollar bill or a five

a ten-dollar bill or a ten

a twenty-dollar bill or a twenty

20

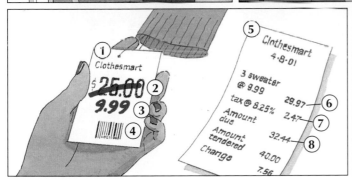

| | | | |
|---|---|---|---|
| **A. shop** for | **E. keep** | **2.** regular price | **6.** price/cost |
| **B. sell** | **F. return** | **3.** sale price | **7.** sales tax |
| **C. pay** for/**buy** | **G. exchange** | **4.** bar code | **8.** total |
| **D. give** | **1.** price tag | **5.** receipt | **9.** change |

## More vocabulary

When you use a credit card to shop, you get a **bill** in the mail. Bills list, in writing, the items you bought and the total you have to pay.

## Share your answers.

1. Name three things you pay for every month.
2. Name one thing you will buy this week.
3. Where do you like to shop?

# Age and Physical Description

1. children

2. baby

3. toddler

4. 6-year-old boy

5. 10-year-old girl

6. teenagers

7. 13-year-old boy

8. 19-year-old girl

9. adults

10. woman

11. man

12. senior citizen

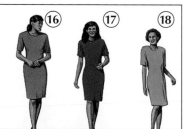

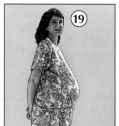

13. young

14. middle-aged

15. elderly

16. tall

17. average height

18. short

19. pregnant

20. heavyset

21. average weight

22. thin/slim

23. attractive

24. cute

25. physically challenged

26. sight impaired/blind

27. hearing impaired/deaf

**Talk about yourself and your teacher.**

*I am <u>young</u>, <u>average height</u>, and <u>average weight</u>.*

*My teacher is <u>a middle-aged</u>, <u>tall</u>, <u>thin</u> man.*

**Use the new language.**

Turn to **Hobbies and Games,** pages **162–163.**

Describe each person on the page.

*He's <u>a heavyset</u>, <u>short</u>, <u>senior citizen</u>.*

Trends Hair Salon
NO APPT. NECESSARY

SHAMPOO
BLOW DRY
CUT

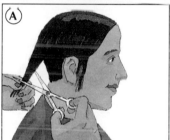
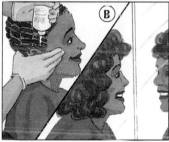

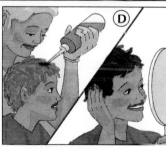

| | | | |
|---|---|---|---|
| **1.** short hair | **8.** bangs | **15.** black hair | **22.** comb |
| **2.** shoulder-length hair | **9.** straight hair | **16.** blond hair | **A. cut** hair |
| **3.** long hair | **10.** wavy hair | **17.** brown hair | **B. perm** hair |
| **4.** part | **11.** curly hair | **18.** brush | **C. set** hair |
| **5.** mustache | **12.** bald | **19.** scissors | **D. color** hair/**dye** hair |
| **6.** beard | **13.** gray hair | **20.** blow dryer | |
| **7.** sideburns | **14.** red hair | **21.** rollers | |

**More vocabulary**

**hair stylist:** a person who cuts, sets, and perms hair
**hair salon:** the place where a hair stylist works

**Talk about your hair.**

*My hair is <u>long</u>, <u>straight</u>, and <u>brown</u>.*
*I have <u>long</u>, <u>straight</u>, <u>brown</u> hair.*
*When I was a child my hair was <u>short</u>, <u>curly</u>, and <u>blond</u>.*

*Tom Lee's Family*

**1.** grandparents

Min

Lu

**2.** grandmother   **3.** grandfather

**4.** parents

Rose

Chang

Helen

Daniel

**5.** mother   **6.** father

**10.** aunt   **11.** uncle

Tom

Lily

Alex

Emily

**8.** sister   **9.** brother

**12.** cousin

**7.** (Min and Lu's) grandson

Berta

Mario

*Ana Garcia's Family*

**13.** mother-in-law   **14.** father-in-law

Ana

Marta

Carlos

Tito

**20.** (Tito's) wife

**15.** sister-in-law   **16.** brother-in-law

**19.** husband

Alice

Eddie

Sara

Felix

**17.** niece   **18.** nephew

**21.** daughter   **22.** son

**More vocabulary**

Lily and Emily are Min and Lu's **granddaughters.**

Daniel is Min and Lu's **son-in-law.**

Ana is Berta and Mario's **daughter-in-law.**

**Share your answers.**

1. How many brothers and sisters do you have?
2. What number son or daughter are you?
3. Do you have any children?

## Lisa Smith's Family

**23.** married

Carol     Dan

Lisa

**24.** divorced

**25.** single mother

**26.** single father

Rick     Carol

**27.** remarried

Dan     Sue

Rick     Carol

**28.** stepfather

David     Mary

**29.** half brother     **30.** half sister

Lisa

Dan     Sue

**31.** stepmother

Kim     Bill

**32.** stepsister     **33.** stepbrother

---

**More vocabulary**

Carol is Dan's **former wife**.

Sue is Dan's **wife**.

Dan is Carol's **former husband**.

Rick is Carol's **husband**.

Lisa is the **stepdaughter** of both Rick and Sue.

# Daily Routines

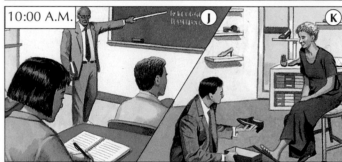

A. **wake up**

B. **get up**

C. **take** a shower

D. **get dressed**

E. **eat** breakfast

F. **make** lunch

G. **take** the children to school

H. **take** the bus to school

I. **drive** to work / **go** to work

J. **be** in school

K. **work**

L. **go** to the market

M. **leave** work

**Grammar point:** 3rd person singular

For **he** and **she**, we add **-s** or **-es** to the verb.

*He/She wakes up.*

*He/She watches TV.*

These verbs are different (irregular):

be      *He/She **is** in school at 10:00 a.m.*

have     *He/She **has** dinner at 6:30 p.m.*

5:30 P.M. — N, O

6:00 P.M. — P, Q

6:30 P.M. — R

7:30 P.M. — S, T

8:00 P.M. — U, V

8:30 P.M. — W

10:30 P.M. — X

11:00 P.M. — Y

**N. clean** the house

**O. pick up** the children

**P. cook** dinner

**Q. come** home / **get** home

**R. have** dinner

**S. watch** TV

**T. do** homework

**U. relax**

**V. read** the paper

**W. exercise**

**X. go** to bed

**Y. go** to sleep

**Talk about your daily routine.**

*I take a shower in the morning.*
*I go to school in the evening.*
*I go to bed at 11 o'clock.*

**Share your answers.**

1. Who makes dinner in your family?
2. Who goes to the market?
3. Who goes to work?

**A. be born**

**B. start** school

**C. immigrate**

**D. graduate**

**E. learn** to drive

**F. join** the army

**G. get** a job

**H. become** a citizen

**I. rent** an apartment

**J. go** to college

**K. fall in love**

**L. get married**

**Grammar point:** past tense

| start<br>learn<br>join<br>rent<br>travel | +ed | immigrate<br>graduate<br>move<br>retire<br>die | +d |
| --- | --- | --- | --- |

These verbs are different (irregular):

| be | — was | have — had |
| --- | --- | --- |
| get | — got | buy — bought |
| become | — became | |
| go | — went | |
| fall | — fell | |

**M. have** a baby

**N. travel**

1960 | 1967

**O. buy** a house

**P. move**

1971 | 1971

**Q. have** a grandchild

**R. die**

1985 | 1997

**1.** birth certificate

**2.** diploma

**3.** Resident Alien card

**4.** driver's license

**5.** Social Security card

**6.** Certificate of Naturalization

**7.** college degree

**8.** marriage license

**9.** passport

## More vocabulary

When a husband dies, his wife becomes a **widow**.
When a wife dies, her husband becomes a **widower**.
When older people stop working, we say they **retire**.

## Talk about yourself.

*I was born in 1968.*
*I learned to drive in 1987.*
*I immigrated in 1990.*

# Feelings

1. hot
2. thirsty
3. sleepy

4. cold
5. hungry
6. full

7. comfortable
8. uncomfortable
9. disgusted
10. calm
11. nervous

12. in pain
13. worried
14. sick
15. well
16. relieved

17. hurt
18. lonely
19. in love

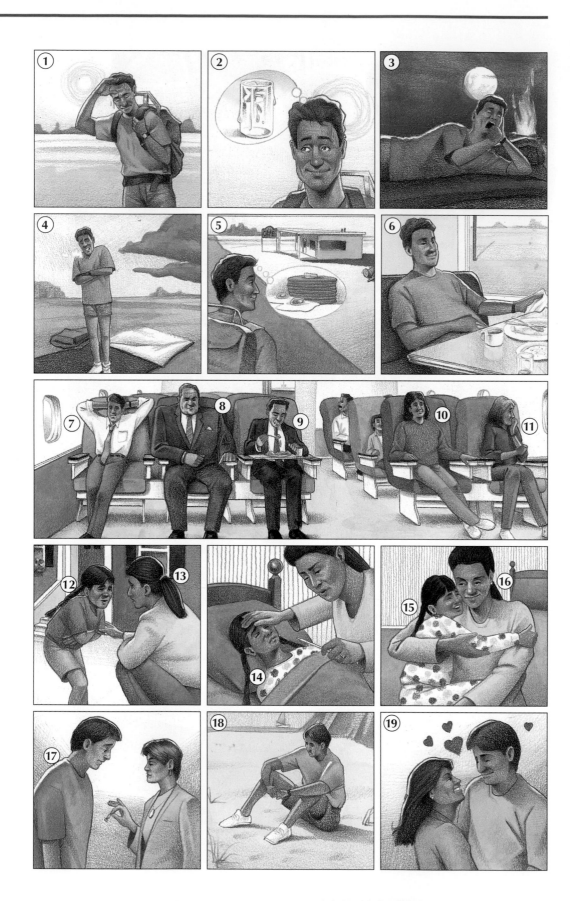

**More vocabulary**

**furious:** very angry
**terrified:** very scared
**overjoyed:** very happy

**exhausted:** very tired
**starving:** very hungry
**humiliated:** very embarrassed

**Talk about your feelings.**

*I feel <u>happy</u> when I see <u>my friends</u>.*
*I feel <u>homesick</u> when I think about <u>my family</u>.*

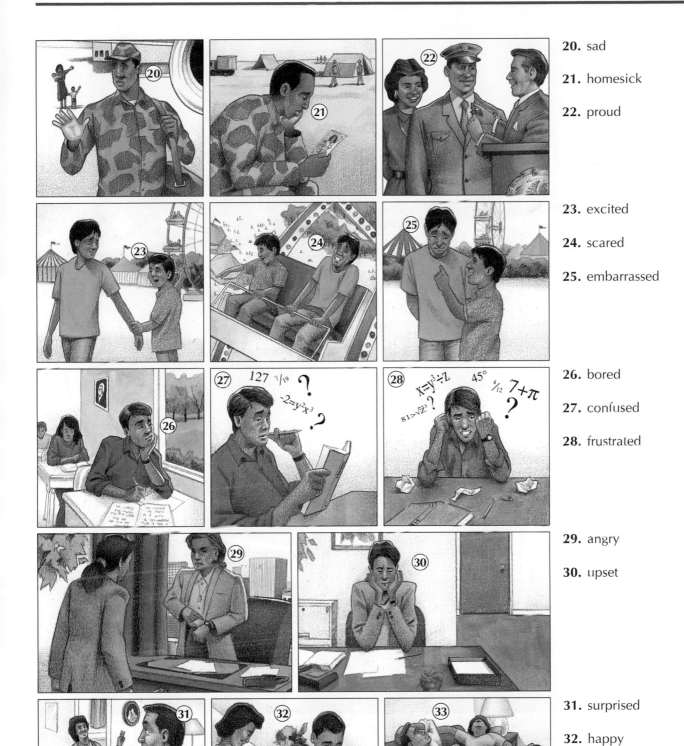

20. sad

21. homesick

22. proud

23. excited

24. scared

25. embarrassed

26. bored

27. confused

28. frustrated

29. angry

30. upset

31. surprised

32. happy

33. tired

**Use the new language.**

Look at **Clothing I,** page **64,** and answer the questions.

1. How does the runner feel?

2. How does the man at the bus stop feel?

3. How does the woman at the bus stop feel?

4. How do the teenagers feel?

5. How does the little boy feel?

# A Graduation

The Ceremony

| 1. graduating class | 5. podium | 9. guest speaker | B. **applaud / clap** |
| 2. gown | 6. graduate | 10. audience | C. **cry** |
| 3. cap | 7. diploma | 11. photographer | D. **take** a picture |
| 4. stage | 8. valedictorian | A. **graduate** | E. **give** a speech |

**Talk about what the people in the pictures are doing.**

She is
- tak**ing** a picture.
- giv**ing** a speech.
- smil**ing**.
- laugh**ing**.

He is
- mak**ing** a toast.
- clap**ping**.

They are
- graduat**ing**.
- hug**ging**.
- kiss**ing**.
- applaud**ing**.

32

The Party

| | | | |
|---|---|---|---|
| **12.** caterer | **15.** banner | **18.** gifts | **H. laugh** |
| **13.** buffet | **16.** dance floor | **F. kiss** | **I. make a toast** |
| **14.** guests | **17.** DJ (disc jockey) | **G. hug** | **J. dance** |

**Share your answers.**

1. Did you ever go to a graduation? Whose?
2. Did you ever give a speech? Where?
3. Did you ever hear a great speaker? Where?

4. Did you ever go to a graduation party?
5. What do you like to eat at parties?
6. Do you like to dance at parties?

**1.** the city/an urban area    **2.** the suburbs    **3.** a small town    **4.** the country/a rural area

**5.** apartment building

**6.** house

**7.** townhouse

**8.** mobile home

**9.** college dormitory

**10.** shelter

**11.** nursing home

**12.** ranch

**13.** farm

**More vocabulary**

**duplex house:** a house divided into two homes

**condominium:** an apartment building where each apartment is owned separately

**co-op:** an apartment building owned by the residents

**Share your answers.**

1. Do you like where you live?
2. Where did you live in your country?
3. What types of housing are there near your school?

## Renting an apartment

A. **look for** a new apartment

Utilities?

Utilities are included.

B. **talk** to the manager

RENTAL AGREEMENT

C. **sign** a rental agreement

D. **move in**

E. **unpack**

F. **pay** the rent

## Buying a house

G. **talk** to the Realtor

$$$$$$

H. **make** an offer

Congratulations!

STATE BANK

I. **get** a loan

J. **take** ownership

K. **arrange** the furniture

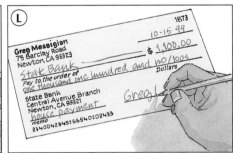

L. **pay** the mortgage

---

**More vocabulary**

**lease:** a rental agreement for a specific period of time

**utilities:** gas, water, and electricity for the home

**Practice talking to an apartment manager.**

*How much is the rent?*

*Are utilities included?*

*When can I move in?*

Entrance

Laundry Room

Recreation Room

Garage

**1.** first floor

**2.** second floor

**3.** third floor

**4.** fourth floor

**5.** roof garden

**6.** playground

**7.** fire escape

**8.** intercom / speaker

**9.** security system

**10.** doorman

**11.** vacancy sign

**12.** manager / superintendent

**13.** security gate

**14.** storage locker

**15.** parking space

**More vocabulary**

**rec room**: a short way of saying **recreation room**

**basement**: the area below the street level of an apartment or a house

**Talk about where you live.**

*I live in Apartment 3 near the entrance.*

*I live in Apartment 11 on the second floor near the fire escape.*

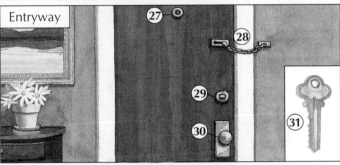

**16.** swimming pool

**17.** balcony

**18.** courtyard

**19.** air conditioner

**20.** trash bin

**21.** alley

**22.** neighbor

**23.** fire exit

**24.** trash chute

**25.** smoke detector

**26.** stairway

**27.** peephole

**28.** door chain

**29.** dead-bolt lock

**30.** doorknob

**31.** key

**32.** landlord

**33.** tenant

**34.** elevator

**35.** stairs

**36.** mailboxes

**Grammar point: *there is, there are***
singular: *there is*   plural: *there are*
***There is*** *a fire exit in the hallway.*
***There are*** *mailboxes in the lobby.*

**Talk about apartments.**
*My apartment has* <u>an elevator</u>, <u>a lobby</u>, *and* <u>a rec room</u>.
*My apartment doesn't have* <u>a pool</u> *or* <u>a garage</u>.
*My apartment needs* <u>air conditioning</u>.

# A House

| 1. floor plan | 7. garage door | 13. steps | 19. gutter |
| 2. backyard | 8. screen door | 14. front walk | 20. roof |
| 3. fence | 9. porch light | 15. front yard | 21. chimney |
| 4. mailbox | 10. doorbell | 16. deck | 22. TV antenna |
| 5. driveway | 11. front door | 17. window | |
| 6. garage | 12. storm door | 18. shutter | |

**More vocabulary**

**two-story house:** a house with two floors

**downstairs:** the bottom floor

**upstairs:** the part of a house above the bottom floor

**Share your answers.**

1. What do you like about this house?
2. What's something you don't like about the house?
3. Describe the perfect house.

| | | | |
|---|---|---|---|
| **1.** hedge | **8.** sprinkler | **15.** pruning shears | **22.** lawn mower |
| **2.** hammock | **9.** hose | **16.** wheelbarrow | **A.** **weed** the flower bed |
| **3.** garbage can | **10.** compost pile | **17.** watering can | **B.** **water** the plants |
| **4.** leaf blower | **11.** rake | **18.** flowerpot | **C.** **mow** the lawn |
| **5.** patio furniture | **12.** hedge clippers | **19.** flower | **D.** **plant** a tree |
| **6.** patio | **13.** shovel | **20.** bush | **E.** **trim** the hedge |
| **7.** barbecue grill | **14.** trowel | **21.** lawn | **F.** **rake** the leaves |

**Talk about your yard and gardening.**

*I like to plant trees.*

*I don't like to weed.*

*I like/don't like to work in the yard/garden.*

**Share your answers.**

1. What flowers, trees, or plants do you see in the picture? (Look at **Trees, Plants, and Flowers,** pages **128–129** for help.)

2. Do you ever use a barbecue grill to cook?

| | | | |
|---|---|---|---|
| **1.** cabinet | **8.** shelf | **15.** toaster oven | **22.** counter |
| **2.** paper towels | **9.** refrigerator | **16.** pot | **23.** drawer |
| **3.** dish drainer | **10.** freezer | **17.** teakettle | **24.** pan |
| **4.** dishwasher | **11.** coffeemaker | **18.** stove | **25.** electric mixer |
| **5.** garbage disposal | **12.** blender | **19.** burner | **26.** food processor |
| **6.** sink | **13.** microwave oven | **20.** oven | **27.** cutting board |
| **7.** toaster | **14.** electric can opener | **21.** broiler | |

**Talk about the location of kitchen items.**

*The toaster oven* is <u>on the counter</u> *near the stove*.
*The microwave* is <u>above the stove</u>.

**Share your answers.**

1. Do you have a garbage disposal? a dishwasher? a microwave?
2. Do you eat in the kitchen?

| | | | |
|---|---|---|---|
| **1.** china cabinet | **8.** candlestick | **15.** pepper shaker | **22.** knife |
| **2.** set of dishes | **9.** vase | **16.** dining room chair | **23.** spoon |
| **3.** platter | **10.** tray | **17.** dining room table | **24.** plate |
| **4.** ceiling fan | **11.** teapot | **18.** tablecloth | **25.** bowl |
| **5.** light fixture | **12.** sugar bowl | **19.** napkin | **26.** glass |
| **6.** serving dish | **13.** creamer | **20.** place mat | **27.** coffee cup |
| **7.** candle | **14.** saltshaker | **21.** fork | **28.** mug |

**Practice asking for things in the dining room.**

*Please pass the platter.*

*May I have the creamer?*

*Could I have a fork, please?*

**Share your answers.**

1. What are the women in the picture saying?
2. In your home, where do you eat?
3. Do you like to make dinner for your friends?

# A Living Room

| | | | |
|---|---|---|---|
| **1.** bookcase | **8.** mantel | **15.** floor lamp | **22.** magazine holder |
| **2.** basket | **9.** fireplace | **16.** drapes | **23.** coffee table |
| **3.** track lighting | **10.** fire | **17.** window | **24.** armchair/easy chair |
| **4.** lightbulb | **11.** fire screen | **18.** plant | **25.** love seat |
| **5.** ceiling | **12.** logs | **19.** sofa/couch | **26.** TV (television) |
| **6.** wall | **13.** wall unit | **20.** throw pillow | **27.** carpet |
| **7.** painting | **14.** stereo system | **21.** end table | |

**Use the new language.**

Look at **Colors,** page **12,** and describe this room.

*There is a gray sofa and a gray armchair.*

**Talk about your living room.**

*In my living room I have a sofa, two chairs, and a coffee table.*

*I don't have a fireplace or a wall unit.*

42

| | | | |
|---|---|---|---|
| **1.** hamper | **8.** towel rack | **15.** toilet paper | **22.** sink |
| **2.** bathtub | **9.** tile | **16.** toilet brush | **23.** soap |
| **3.** rubber mat | **10.** showerhead | **17.** toilet | **24.** soap dish |
| **4.** drain | **11.** (mini)blinds | **18.** mirror | **25.** wastebasket |
| **5.** hot water | **12.** bath towel | **19.** medicine cabinet | **26.** scale |
| **6.** faucet | **13.** hand towel | **20.** toothbrush | **27.** bath mat |
| **7.** cold water | **14.** washcloth | **21.** toothbrush holder | |

**More vocabulary**

**half bath:** a bathroom without a shower or bathtub
**linen closet:** a closet or cabinet for towels and sheets
**stall shower:** a shower without a bathtub

**Share your answers.**

1. Do you turn off the water when you brush your teeth?
   wash your hair? shave?
2. Does your bathroom have a bathtub or a stall shower?

43

| | | | |
|---|---|---|---|
| **1.** mirror | **8.** bed | **15.** headboard | **22.** dust ruffle |
| **2.** dresser/bureau | **9.** pillow | **16.** clock radio | **23.** rug |
| **3.** drawer | **10.** pillowcase | **17.** lamp | **24.** floor |
| **4.** closet | **11.** bedspread | **18.** lampshade | **25.** mattress |
| **5.** curtains | **12.** blanket | **19.** light switch | **26.** box spring |
| **6.** window shade | **13.** flat sheet | **20.** outlet | **27.** bed frame |
| **7.** photograph | **14.** fitted sheet | **21.** night table | |

**Use the new language.**

Describe this room. (See **Describing Things**, page **11,** for help.)

*I see a soft pillow and a beautiful bedspread.*

**Share your answers.**

1. What is your favorite thing in your bedroom?
2. Do you have a clock in your bedroom? Where is it?
3. Do you have a mirror in your bedroom? Where is it?

| | | | |
|---|---|---|---|
| 1. bunk bed | 7. bumper pad | 13. diaper pail | 19. cradle |
| 2. comforter | 8. chest of drawers | 14. dollhouse | 20. coloring book |
| 3. night-light | 9. baby monitor | 15. blocks | 21. crayons |
| 4. mobile | 10. teddy bear | 16. ball | 22. puzzle |
| 5. wallpaper | 11. smoke detector | 17. picture book | 23. stuffed animals |
| 6. crib | 12. changing table | 18. doll | 24. toy chest |

**Talk about where items are in the room.**

_The dollhouse is near the coloring book._

_The teddy bear is on the chest of drawers._

**Share your answers.**

1. Do you think this is a good room for children? Why?
2. What toys did you play with when you were a child?
3. What children's stories do you know?

45

**A.** **dust** the furniture

**B.** **recycle** the newspapers

**C.** **clean** the oven

**D.** **wash** the windows

**E.** **sweep** the floor

**F.** **empty** the wastebasket

**G.** **make** the bed

**H.** **put away** the toys

**I.** **vacuum** the carpet

**J.** **mop** the floor

**K.** **polish** the furniture

**L.** **scrub** the floor

**M.** **wash** the dishes

**N.** **dry** the dishes

**O.** **wipe** the counter

**P.** **change** the sheets

**Q.** **take out** the garbage

**Talk about yourself.**

*I wash the dishes every day.*
*I change the sheets every week.*
*I never dry the dishes.*

**Share your answers.**

1. Who does the housework in your family?
2. What is your favorite cleaning job?
3. What is your least favorite cleaning job?

1. feather duster

2. recycling bin

3. oven cleaner

4. rubber gloves

5. steel-wool soap pads

6. rags

7. stepladder

8. glass cleaner

9. squeegee

10. broom

11. dustpan

12. trash bags

13. vacuum cleaner

14. vacuum cleaner attachments

15. vacuum cleaner bag

16. wet mop

17. dust mop

18. furniture polish

19. scrub brush

20. bucket/pail

21. dishwashing liquid

22. dish towel

23. cleanser

24. sponge

**Practice asking for the items.**

*I want to <u>wash the windows</u>.*
*Please hand me <u>the squeegee</u>.*

*I have to <u>sweep the floor</u>.*
*Can you get me <u>the broom</u>, please?*

1. The water heater is **not working**.

2. The power is **out**.

3. The roof is **leaking**.

4. The wall is **cracked**.

5. The window is **broken**.

6. The lock is **broken**.

7. The steps are **broken**.

8. roofer

9. electrician

10. repair person

11. locksmith

12. carpenter

13. fuse box

14. gas meter

**Use the new language.**

Look at **Tools and Building Supplies,** pages **150–151.**
Name the tools you use for household repairs.

*I use <u>a hammer and nails</u> to fix <u>a broken step</u>.*
*I use <u>a wrench</u> to repair <u>a dripping faucet</u>.*

15. The furnace is **broken**.

16. The faucet is **dripping**.

17. The sink is **overflowing**.

18. The toilet is **stopped up**.

19. The pipes are **frozen**.

20. plumber

21. exterminator

## Household pests

22. termite(s)

23. flea(s)

24. ant(s)

25. cockroach(es)

26. mice*

27. rat(s)

*Note: *one mouse, two mice*

## More vocabulary

**fix:** to repair something that is broken

**exterminate:** to kill household pests

**pesticide:** a chemical that is used to kill household pests

## Share your answers.

1. Who does household repairs in your home?

2. What is the worst problem a home can have?

3. What is the most expensive problem a home can have?

# Fruit

| | | | |
|---|---|---|---|
| **1.** grapes | **9.** grapefruit | **17.** strawberries | **25.** dates |
| **2.** pineapples | **10.** oranges | **18.** raspberries | **26.** prunes |
| **3.** bananas | **11.** lemons | **19.** blueberries | **27.** raisins |
| **4.** apples | **12.** limes | **20.** papayas | **28.** not ripe |
| **5.** peaches | **13.** tangerines | **21.** mangoes | **29.** ripe |
| **6.** pears | **14.** avocadoes | **22.** coconuts | **30.** rotten |
| **7.** apricots | **15.** cantaloupes | **23.** nuts | |
| **8.** plums | **16.** cherries | **24.** watermelons | |

**Language note: *a bunch of***

We say *a bunch of grapes* and *a bunch of bananas.*

**Share your answers.**

1. Which fruits do you put in a fruit salad?
2. Which fruits are sold in your area in the summer?
3. What fruits did you have in your country?

TOMATOES
.69/lb.

CORN
4/$1.00

| | | | |
|---|---|---|---|
| **1.** lettuce | **9.** celery | **17.** scallions | **25.** string beans |
| **2.** cabbage | **10.** parsley | **18.** eggplants | **26.** mushrooms |
| **3.** carrots | **11.** spinach | **19.** peas | **27.** corn |
| **4.** zucchini | **12.** cucumbers | **20.** artichokes | **28.** onions |
| **5.** radishes | **13.** squash | **21.** potatoes | **29.** garlic |
| **6.** beets | **14.** turnips | **22.** yams | |
| **7.** sweet peppers | **15.** broccoli | **23.** tomatoes | |
| **8.** chili peppers | **16.** cauliflower | **24.** asparagus | |

**Language note: *a bunch of, a head of***

We say *a bunch of carrots, a bunch of celery,* and *a bunch of spinach.*

We say *a head of lettuce, a head of cabbage,* and *a head of cauliflower.*

**Share your answers.**

**1.** Which vegetables do you eat raw? cooked?

**2.** Which vegetables need to be in the refrigerator?

**3.** Which vegetables don't need to be in the refrigerator?

### Beef

**1.** roast beef

**2.** steak

**3.** stewing beef

**4.** ground beef

**5.** beef ribs

**6.** veal cutlets

**7.** liver

**8.** tripe

### Pork

**9.** ham

**10.** pork chops

**11.** bacon

**12.** sausage

### Lamb

**13.** lamb shanks

**14.** leg of lamb

**15.** lamb chops

**16.** chicken

**17.** turkey

**18.** duck

**19.** breasts

**20.** wings

**21.** thighs

**22.** drumsticks

**23.** gizzards

**24.** **raw** chicken

**25.** **cooked** chicken

### More vocabulary

**vegetarian:** a person who doesn't eat meat

Meat and poultry without bones are called **boneless**.

Poultry without skin is called **skinless**.

### Share your answers.

**1.** What kind of meat do you eat most often?

**2.** What kind of meat do you use in soup?

**3.** What part of the chicken do you like the most?

| | | |
|---|---|---|
| **1.** white bread | **6.** pastrami | **11.** Swiss cheese |
| **2.** wheat bread | **7.** roast beef | **12.** jack cheese |
| **3.** rye bread | **8.** corned beef | **13.** potato salad |
| **4.** smoked turkey | **9.** American cheese | **14.** coleslaw |
| **5.** salami | **10.** cheddar cheese | **15.** pasta salad |

**Fish**

| | |
|---|---|
| **16.** trout | **20.** halibut |
| **17.** catfish | **21.** filet of sole |
| **18.** whole salmon | |
| **19.** salmon steak | |

**Shellfish**

| | |
|---|---|
| **22.** crab | **26.** mussels |
| **23.** lobster | **27.** oysters |
| **24.** shrimp | **28.** clams |
| **25.** scallops | **29.** **fresh** fish |
| | **30.** **frozen** fish |

**Practice ordering a sandwich.**

*I'd like <u>roast beef</u> and <u>American cheese</u> on <u>rye bread</u>.*

**Tell what you want on it.**

*Please put <u>tomato</u>, <u>lettuce</u>, <u>onions</u>, and <u>mustard</u> on it.*

**Share your answers.**

**1.** Do you like to eat fish?

**2.** Do you buy fresh or frozen fish?

53

**1.** bottle return

**2.** meat and poultry section

**3.** shopping cart

**4.** canned goods

**5.** aisle

**6.** baked goods

**7.** shopping basket

**8.** manager

**9.** dairy section

**10.** pet food

**11.** produce section

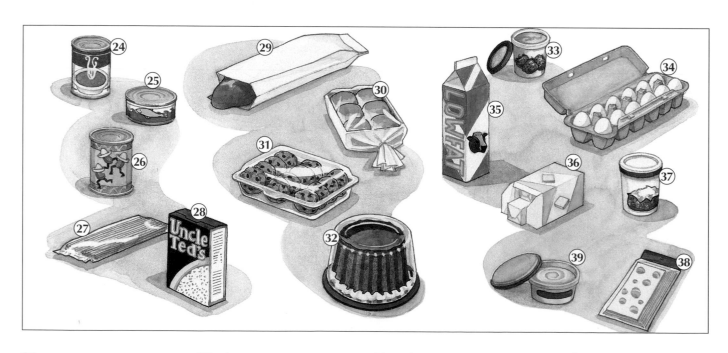

**24.** soup

**25.** tuna

**26.** beans

**27.** spaghetti

**28.** rice

**29.** bread

**30.** rolls

**31.** cookies

**32.** cake

**33.** yogurt

**34.** eggs

**35.** milk

**36.** butter

**37.** sour cream

**38.** cheese

**39.** margarine

| | | | |
|---|---|---|---|
| **12.** frozen foods | **15.** beverages | **18.** cash register | **21.** bagger |
| **13.** baking products | **16.** snack foods | **19.** checker | **22.** paper bag |
| **14.** paper products | **17.** checkstand | **20.** line | **23.** plastic bag |

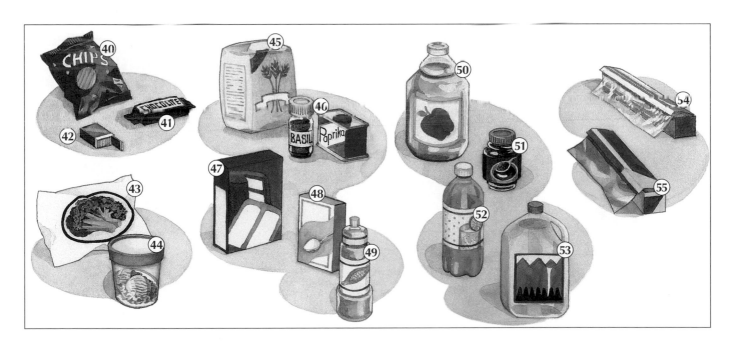

| | | | |
|---|---|---|---|
| **40.** potato chips | **44.** ice cream | **48.** sugar | **52.** soda |
| **41.** candy bar | **45.** flour | **49.** oil | **53.** bottled water |
| **42.** gum | **46.** spices | **50.** apple juice | **54.** plastic wrap |
| **43.** frozen vegetables | **47.** cake mix | **51.** instant coffee | **55.** aluminum foil |

## Containers and Packaged Foods

 **1.** bottle

 **2.** jar

 **3.** can

 **4.** carton

 **5.** container

 **6.** box

 **7.** bag

 **8.** package

 **9.** six-pack

 **10.** loaf

 **11.** roll

 **12.** tube

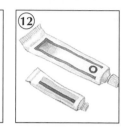

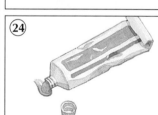

**13.** a bottle of soda

**14.** a jar of jam

**15.** a can of soup

**16.** a carton of eggs

**17.** a container of cottage cheese

**18.** a box of cereal

**19.** a bag of flour

**20.** a package of cookies

**21.** a six-pack of soda

**22.** a loaf of bread

**23.** a roll of paper towels

**24.** a tube of toothpaste

---

**Grammar point: *How much? How many?***

Some foods can be counted: *one apple, two apples.*

***How many** apples do you need? I need **two** apples.*

Some foods cannot be counted, like liquids, grains, spices, or dairy foods. For these, count containers: *one box of rice, two boxes of rice.*

***How much** rice do you need? I need **two** boxes.*

**A. Measure** the ingredients.

**B. Weigh** the food.

**C. Convert** the measurements.

## Liquid measures

1 fl. oz.        1 c.        1 pt.        1 qt.        1 gal.

## Dry measures

1 tsp.        1 TBS.        1/4 c.        1/2 c.        1 c.

## Weight

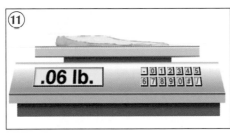

1. a fluid ounce of water

2. a cup of oil

3. a pint of yogurt

4. a quart of milk

5. a gallon of apple juice

6. a teaspoon of salt

7. a tablespoon of sugar

8. a 1/4 cup of brown sugar

9. a 1/2 cup of raisins

10. a cup of flour

11. an ounce of cheese

12. a pound of roast beef

| VOLUME | EQUIVALENCIES | | WEIGHT |
|---|---|---|---|
| 1 fl. oz. = 30 milliliters (ml.) | 3 tsp. = 1 TBS. | 2 c. = 1 pt. | 1 oz. = 28.35 grams (g.) |
| 1 c. = 237 ml. | 2 TBS. = 1 fl. oz. | 2 pt. = 1 qt. | 1 lb. = 453.6 g. |
| 1 pt. = .47 liters (l.) | 8 fl. oz. = 1 c. | 4 qt. = 1 gal. | 2.205 lbs. = 1 kilogram |
| 1 qt. = .95 l. | | | 1 lb. = 16 oz. |
| 1 gal. = 3.79 l. | | | |

## Scrambled eggs

A. **Break** 3 eggs.

B. **Beat** well.

C. **Grease** the pan.

D. **Pour** the eggs into the pan.

E. **Stir.**

F. **Cook** until done.

 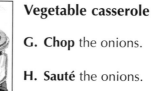 

  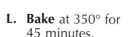

## Vegetable casserole

G. **Chop** the onions.

H. **Sauté** the onions.

I. **Steam** the broccoli.

J. **Grate** the cheese.

K. **Mix** the ingredients.

L. **Bake** at 350° for 45 minutes.

## Chicken soup

M. **Cut up** the chicken.

N. **Peel** the carrots.

O. **Slice** the carrots.

P. **Boil** the chicken.

Q. **Add** the vegetables.

R. **Simmer** for 1 hour.

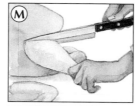  

## Five ways to cook chicken

   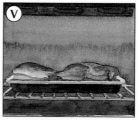 

S.  fry

T.  barbecue / grill

U.  roast

V.  broil

W.  stir-fry

**Talk about the way you prepare these foods.**

I *fry* eggs.

I *bake* potatoes.

**Share your answers.**

1. What are popular ways in your country to make rice? vegetables? meat?

2. What is your favorite way to cook chicken?

**1.** can opener

**2.** grater

**3.** plastic storage container

**4.** steamer

**5.** frying pan

**6.** pot

**7.** ladle

**8.** double boiler

**9.** wooden spoon

**10.** garlic press

**11.** casserole dish

**12.** carving knife

**13.** roasting pan

**14.** roasting rack

**15.** vegetable peeler

**16.** paring knife

**17.** colander

**18.** kitchen timer

**19.** spatula

**20.** eggbeater

**21.** whisk

**22.** strainer

**23.** tongs

**24.** lid

**25.** saucepan

**26.** cake pan

**27.** cookie sheet

**28.** pie pan

**29.** pot holders

**30.** rolling pin

**31.** mixing bowl

**Talk about how to use the utensils.**

*You use a peeler to peel potatoes.*

*You use a pot to cook soup.*

**Use the new language.**

Look at **Food Preparation**, page **58**.

Name the different utensils you see.

| | | | |
|---|---|---|---|
| **1.** hamburger | **8.** green salad | **15.** doughnut | **22.** sugar substitute |
| **2.** french fries | **9.** taco | **16.** salad bar | **23.** ketchup |
| **3.** cheeseburger | **10.** nachos | **17.** lettuce | **24.** mustard |
| **4.** soda | **11.** frozen yogurt | **18.** salad dressing | **25.** mayonnaise |
| **5.** iced tea | **12.** milk shake | **19.** booth | **26.** relish |
| **6.** hot dog | **13.** counter | **20.** straw | **A.** **eat** |
| **7.** pizza | **14.** muffin | **21.** sugar | **B.** **drink** |

**More vocabulary**

**donut:** doughnut (spelling variation)

**condiments:** relish, mustard, ketchup, mayonnaise, etc.

**Share your answers.**

**1.** What would you order at this restaurant?

**2.** Which fast foods are popular in your country?

**3.** How often do you eat fast food? Why?

# Breakfast

# Lunch

# Dinner

# Desserts

# Beverages

1. scrambled eggs

2. sausage

3. toast

4. waffles

5. syrup

6. pancakes

7. bacon

8. grilled cheese sandwich

9. chef's salad

10. soup of the day

11. mashed potatoes

12. roast chicken

13. steak

14. baked potato

15. pasta

16. garlic bread

17. fried fish

18. rice pilaf

19. cake

20. pudding

21. pie

22. coffee

23. decaf coffee

24. tea

**Practice ordering from the menu.**

*I'd like a grilled cheese sandwich and some soup.*

*I'll have the chef's salad and a cup of decaf coffee.*

**Use the new language.**

Look at **Fruit,** page **50.**

Order a slice of pie using the different fruit flavors.

*Please give me a slice of apple pie.*

# A Restaurant

**1.** hostess

**2.** dining room

**3.** menu

**4.** server/waiter

**5.** patron/diner

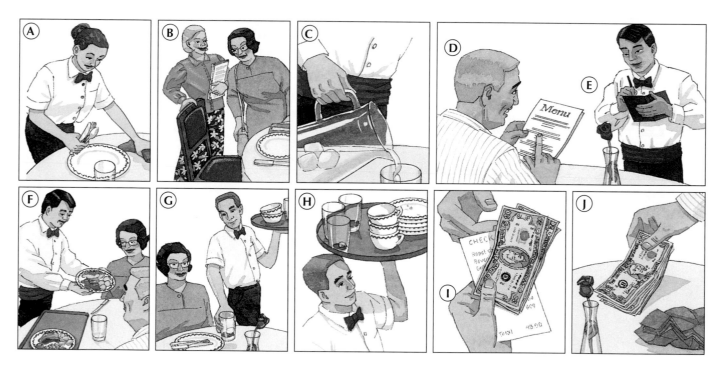

**A.** **set** the table

**B.** **seat** the customer

**C.** **pour** the water

**D.** **order** from the menu

**E.** **take** the order

**F.** **serve** the meal

**G.** **clear** the table

**H.** **carry** the tray

**I.** **pay** the check

**J.** **leave** a tip

## More vocabulary

**eat out:** to go to a restaurant to eat

**take out:** to buy food at a restaurant and take it home to eat

## Practice giving commands.

*Please <u>set the table</u>.*

*I'd like you to <u>clear the table</u>.*

*It's time to <u>serve the meal</u>.*

**6.** server / waitress

**7.** dessert tray

**8.** bread basket

**9.** busperson

**10.** kitchen

**11.** chef

**12.** dishroom

**13.** dishwasher

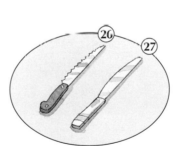
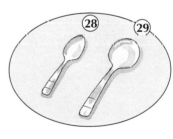

**14.** place setting

**15.** dinner plate

**16.** bread-and-butter plate

**17.** salad plate

**18.** soup bowl

**19.** water glass

**20.** wine glass

**21.** cup

**22.** saucer

**23.** napkin

**24.** salad fork

**25.** dinner fork

**26.** steak knife

**27.** knife

**28.** teaspoon

**29.** soupspoon

**Talk about how you set the table in your home.**

*The glass is on the right.*

*The fork goes on the left.*

*The napkin is next to the plate.*

**Share your answers.**

1. Do you know anyone who works in a restaurant? What does he or she do?

2. In your opinion, which restaurant jobs are hard? Why?

# Clothing I

1. three-piece suit

2. suit

3. dress

4. shirt

5. jeans

6. sports coat

7. turtleneck

8. slacks/pants

9. blouse

10. skirt

11. pullover sweater

12. T-shirt

13. shorts

14. sweatshirt

15. sweatpants

**More vocabulary:**

**outfit:** clothes that look nice together

When clothes are popular, they are **in fashion.**

**Talk about what you're wearing today and what you wore yesterday.**

*I'm wearing* <u>*a gray sweater*</u>, <u>*a red T-shirt*</u>, *and* <u>*blue jeans*</u>.

*Yesterday I wore* <u>*a green pullover sweater*</u>, <u>*a white shirt*</u>, *and* <u>*black slacks*</u>.

| | | |
|---|---|---|
| **16.** jumpsuit | **21.** overalls | **26.** sports shirt |
| **17.** uniform | **22.** tunic | **27.** cardigan sweater |
| **18.** jumper | **23.** leggings | **28.** tuxedo |
| **19.** maternity dress | **24.** vest | **29.** evening gown |
| **20.** knit shirt | **25.** split skirt | |

**Use the new language.**

Look at **A Graduation**, pages **32–33**.

Name the clothes you see.

*The man at the podium is wearing <u>a suit</u>.*

**Share your answers.**

**1.** Which clothes in this picture are in fashion now?

**2.** Who is the best-dressed person in this line? Why?

**3.** What do you wear when you go to the movies?

# Clothing II

| | |
|---|---|
| **1.** hat | **5.** gloves |
| **2.** overcoat | **6.** cap |
| **3.** leather jacket | **7.** jacket |
| **4.** wool scarf/muffler | |

| | |
|---|---|
| **8.** parka | **12.** earmuffs |
| **9.** mittens | **13.** down vest |
| **10.** ski cap | **14.** ski mask |
| **11.** tights | **15.** down jacket |

| | |
|---|---|
| **16.** umbrella | **20.** trench coat |
| **17.** raincoat | **21.** sunglasses |
| **18.** poncho | **22.** swimming trunks |
| **19.** rain boots | **23.** straw hat |

| |
|---|
| **24.** windbreaker |
| **25.** cover-up |
| **26.** swimsuit/bathing suit |
| **27.** baseball cap |

**Use the new language.**

Look at **Weather,** page **10.**

Name the clothing for each weather condition.

*Wear a jacket when it's windy.*

**Share your answers.**

**1.** Which is better in the rain, an umbrella or a poncho?

**2.** Which is better in the cold, a parka or a down jacket?

**3.** Do you have more summer clothes or winter clothes?

| | | | |
|---|---|---|---|
| **1.** leotard | **3.** bike shorts | **4.** pajamas | **7.** blanket sleeper |
| **2.** tank top | | **5.** nightgown | **8.** bathrobe |
| | | **6.** slippers | **9.** nightshirt |

| | | |
|---|---|---|
| **10.** undershirt | **16.** (bikini) panties | **22.** full slip |
| **11.** long underwear | **17.** briefs / underpants | **23.** half slip |
| **12.** boxer shorts | **18.** girdle | **24.** knee-highs |
| **13.** briefs | **19.** garter belt | **25.** kneesocks |
| **14.** athletic supporter / jockstrap | **20.** bra | **26.** stockings |
| **15.** socks | **21.** camisole | **27.** pantyhose |

## More vocabulary

**lingerie:** underwear or sleepwear for women

**loungewear:** clothing (sometimes sleepwear) people wear around the home

## Share your answers.

1. What do you wear when you exercise?
2. What kind of clothing do you wear for sleeping?

# Shoes and Accessories

**1.** salesclerk

**2.** suspenders

**3.** shoe department

**4.** silk scarves*

**5.** hats

**12.** sole

**13.** heel

**14.** shoelace

**15.** toe

**16.** pumps

**17.** high heels

**18.** boots

**19.** loafers

**20.** oxfords

**21.** hiking boots

**22.** tennis shoes

**23.** athletic shoes

**24.** sandals

*\*Note: one scarf, two scarves*

**Talk about the shoes you're wearing today.**

*I'm wearing a pair of <u>white sandals</u>.*

**Practice asking a salesperson for help.**

*Could I try on these <u>sandals</u> in size <u>10</u>?*

*Do you have any <u>silk scarves</u>?*

*Where are <u>the hats</u>?*

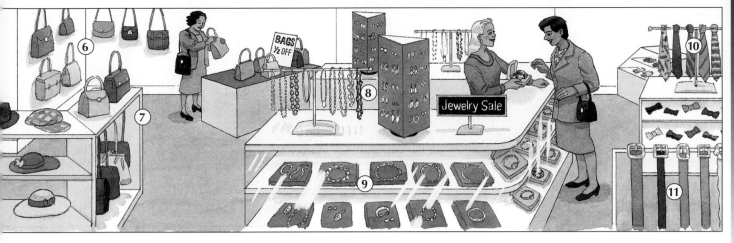

**6.** purses / handbags

**7.** display case

**8.** jewelry

**9.** necklaces

**10.** ties

**11.** belts

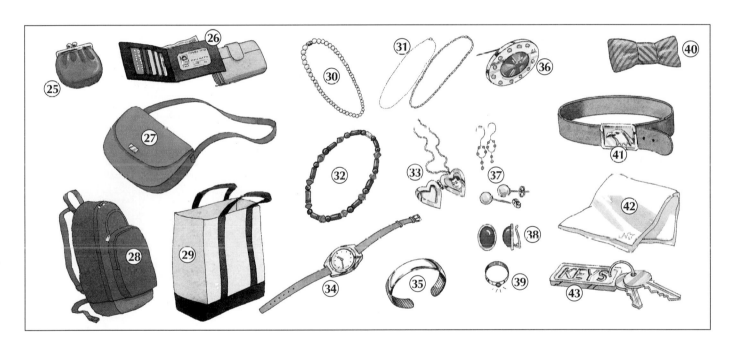

**25.** change purse

**26.** wallet

**27.** shoulder bag

**28.** backpack/bookbag

**29.** tote bag

**30.** string of pearls

**31.** chain

**32.** beads

**33.** locket

**34.** (wrist)watch

**35.** bracelet

**36.** pin

**37.** pierced earrings

**38.** clip-on earrings

**39.** ring

**40.** bow tie

**41.** belt buckle

**42.** handkerchief

**43.** key chain

---

**Share your answers.**

**1.** Which of these accessories are usually worn by women? by men?

**2.** Which of these do you wear every day?

**3.** Which of these would you wear to a job interview? Why?

**4.** Which accessory would you like to receive as a present? Why?

# Describing Clothes

## Sizes

**1.** extra small    **2.** small    **3.** medium    **4.** large    **5.** extra large

## Patterns

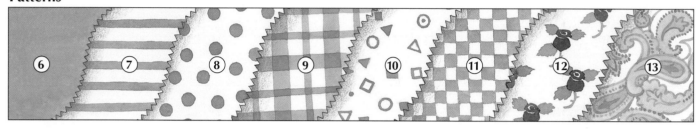

**6.** solid green    **8.** polka-dotted    **10.** print    **12.** floral

**7.** striped    **9.** plaid    **11.** checked    **13.** paisley

## Types of material

**14. wool** sweater    **16. cotton** T-shirt    **18. leather** boots

**15. silk** scarf    **17. linen** jacket    **19. nylon** stockings*

## Problems

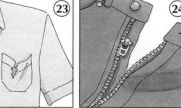

**20.** too small    **22.** stain    **24. broken** zipper

**21.** too big    **23.** rip / tear    **25. missing** button

*Note: Nylon, polyester, rayon, and plastic are synthetic materials.

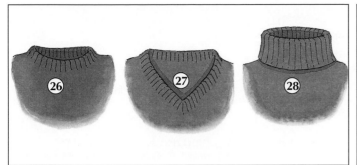

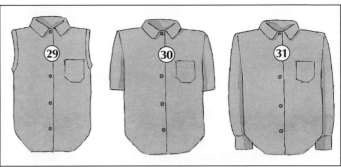

**26. crewneck** sweater      **28. turtleneck** sweater      **30. short-sleeved** shirt

**27. V-neck** sweater      **29. sleeveless** shirt      **31. long-sleeved** shirt

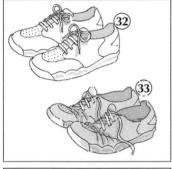 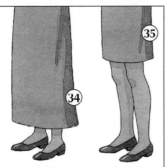  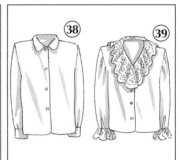

  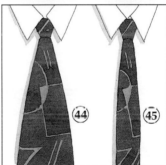 

| | | |
|---|---|---|
| **32. new** shoes | **38. plain** blouse | **44. wide** tie |
| **33. old** shoes | **39. fancy** blouse | **45. narrow** tie |
| **34. long** skirt | **40. light** jacket | **46. low** heels |
| **35. short** skirt | **41. heavy** jacket | **47. high** heels |
| **36. formal** dress | **42. loose** pants / **baggy** pants | |
| **37. casual** dress | **43. tight** pants | |

**Talk about yourself.**

*I like <u>long-sleeved</u> shirts and <u>baggy</u> pants.*
*I like <u>short skirts</u> and <u>high heels</u>.*
*I usually wear <u>plain</u> clothes.*

**Share your answers.**

1. What type of material do you usually wear in the summer? in the winter?
2. What patterns do you see around you?
3. Are you wearing casual or formal clothes?

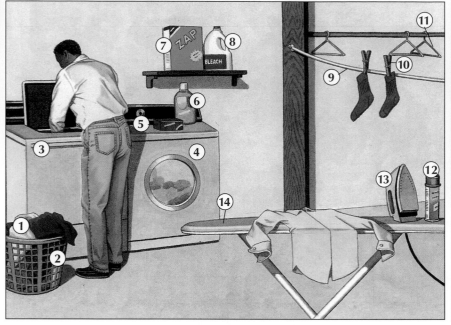

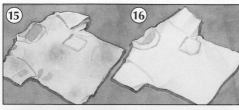
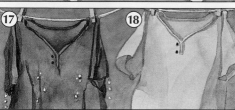

1. laundry
2. laundry basket
3. washer
4. dryer
5. dryer sheets

6. fabric softener
7. laundry detergent
8. bleach
9. clothesline
10. clothespin

11. hanger
12. spray starch
13. iron
14. ironing board
15. **dirty** T-shirt

16. **clean** T-shirt
17. **wet** T-shirt
18. **dry** T-shirt
19. **wrinkled** shirt
20. **ironed** shirt

A. **Sort** the laundry.

B. **Add** the detergent.

C. **Load** the washer.

D. **Clean** the lint trap.

E. **Unload** the dryer.

F. **Fold** the laundry.

G. **Iron** the clothes.

H. **Hang up** the clothes.

### More vocabulary

**dry cleaners:** a business that cleans clothes using chemicals, not water and detergent

 wash in cold water only

 no bleach

 line dry

 dry-clean only, do not wash

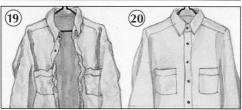

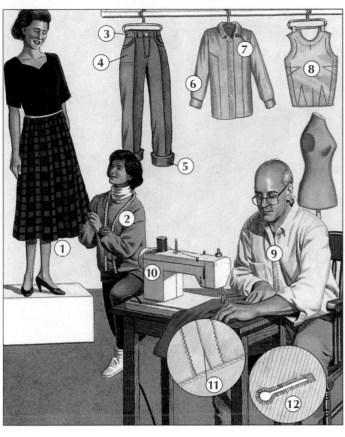

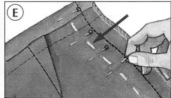

**A. sew** by hand

**B. sew** by machine

**C. lengthen**

**D. shorten**

**E. take in**

**F. let out**

| | | | |
|---|---|---|---|
| **1.** hemline | **4.** pocket | **7.** collar | **10.** sewing machine |
| **2.** dressmaker | **5.** cuff | **8.** pattern | **11.** seam |
| **3.** waistband | **6.** sleeve | **9.** tailor | **12.** buttonhole |

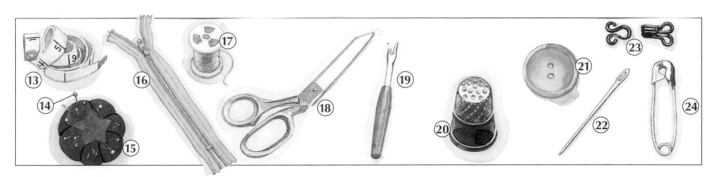

| | | | |
|---|---|---|---|
| **13.** tape measure | **16.** zipper | **19.** seam ripper | **22.** needle |
| **14.** pin | **17.** spool of thread | **20.** thimble | **23.** hook and eye |
| **15.** pin cushion | **18.** (pair of) scissors | **21.** button | **24.** safety pin |

## More vocabulary

**pattern maker:** a person who makes patterns

**garment worker:** a person who works in a clothing factory

**fashion designer:** a person who makes original clothes

## Share your answers.

1. Do you know how to use a sewing machine?
2. Can you sew by hand?

# The Body

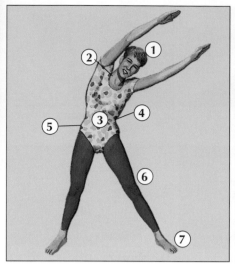

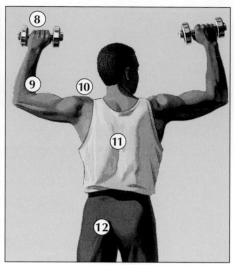

| | | |
|---|---|---|
| **1.** head | **7.** foot | **13.** chest |
| **2.** neck | **8.** hand | **14.** breast |
| **3.** abdomen | **9.** arm | **15.** elbow |
| **4.** waist | **10.** shoulder | **16.** thigh |
| **5.** hip | **11.** back | **17.** knee |
| **6.** leg | **12.** buttocks | **18.** calf |

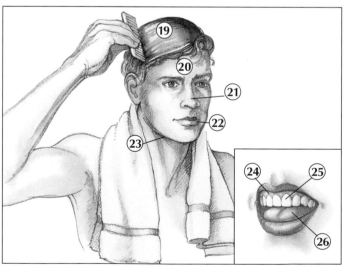

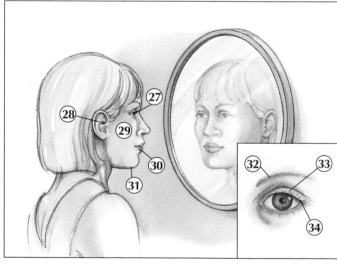

| | | | |
|---|---|---|---|
| **The face** | **23.** jaw | **27.** eye | **32.** eyebrow |
| **19.** hair | **24.** gums | **28.** ear | **33.** eyelid |
| **20.** forehead | **25.** teeth | **29.** cheek | **34.** eyelashes |
| **21.** nose | **26.** tongue | **30.** lip | |
| **22.** mouth | | **31.** chin | |

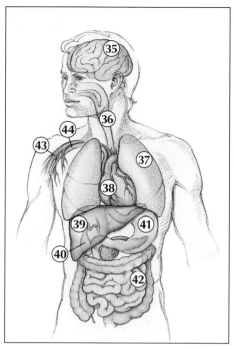

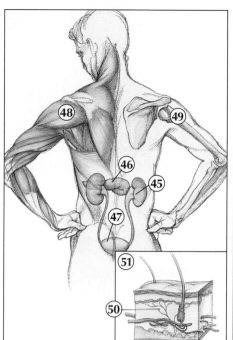

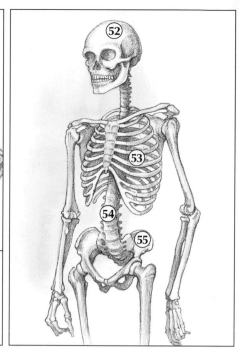

## Inside the body

**35.** brain

**36.** throat

**37.** lung

**38.** heart

**39.** liver

**40.** gallbladder

**41.** stomach

**42.** intestines

**43.** artery

**44.** vein

**45.** kidney

**46.** pancreas

**47.** bladder

**48.** muscle

**49.** bone

**50.** nerve

**51.** skin

## The skeleton

**52.** skull

**53.** rib cage

**54.** spinal column

**55.** pelvis

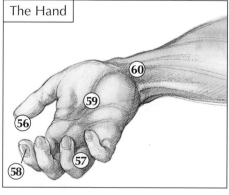

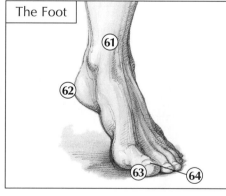

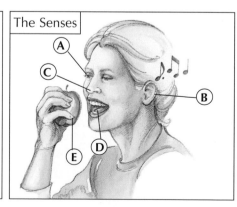

**56.** thumb

**57.** fingers

**58.** fingernail

**59.** palm

**60.** wrist

**61.** ankle

**62.** heel

**63.** toe

**64.** toenail

**A.** see

**B.** hear

**C.** smell

**D.** taste

**E.** touch

# Personal Hygiene

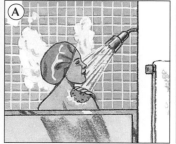   

**A. take** a shower     **B. bathe / take** a bath     **C. use** deodorant     **D. put on** sunscreen

1. shower cap
2. soap
3. bath powder / talcum powder

4. deodorant
5. perfume / cologne
6. sunscreen

7. body lotion
8. moisturizer

 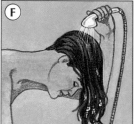   

**E. wash**…hair     **F. rinse**…hair     **G. comb**…hair     **H. dry**…hair     **I. brush**…hair

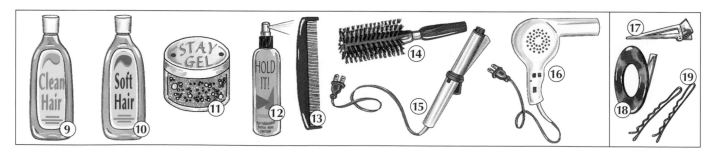

9. shampoo
10. conditioner
11. hair gel

12. hair spray
13. comb
14. brush

15. curling iron
16. blow dryer
17. hair clip

18. barrette
19. bobby pins

**J. brush**…teeth

**K. floss**…teeth

**L. gargle**

**M. shave**

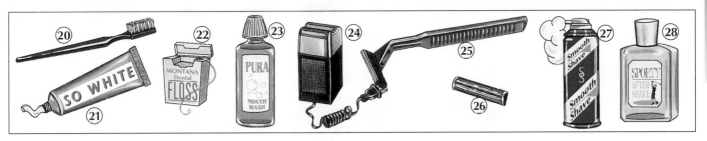

**20.** toothbrush

**21.** toothpaste

**22.** dental floss

**23.** mouthwash

**24.** electric shaver

**25.** razor

**26.** razor blade

**27.** shaving cream

**28.** aftershave

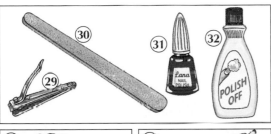

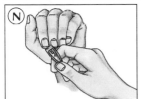

**N. cut**…nails

**O. polish**…nails

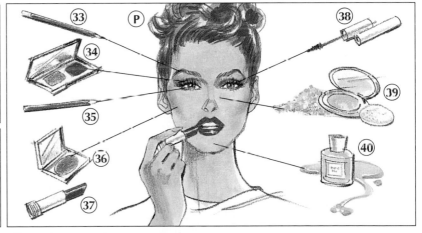

**P. put on**…makeup

**29.** nail clipper

**30.** emery board

**31.** nail polish

**32.** nail polish remover

**33.** eyebrow pencil

**34.** eye shadow

**35.** eyeliner

**36.** blush / rouge

**37.** lipstick

**38.** mascara

**39.** face powder

**40.** foundation

---

## More vocabulary

A product without perfume or scent is **unscented.**

A product that is better for people with allergies is **hypoallergenic.**

## Share your answers.

1. What is your morning routine if you stay home? if you go out?

2. Do women in your culture wear makeup? How old are they when they begin to use it?

# Symptoms and Injuries

1. headache
2. toothache
3. earache
4. stomachache
5. backache

6. sore throat
7. nasal congestion
8. fever/temperature
9. chills
10. rash

A. **cough**
B. **sneeze**
C. **feel** dizzy
D. **feel** nauseous
E. **throw up/vomit**

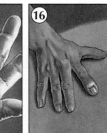

11. insect bite
12. bruise
13. cut

14. sunburn
15. blister
16. **swollen** finger

17. **bloody** nose
18. **sprained** ankle

**Use the new language.**

Look at **Health Care,** pages **80–81.**

Tell what medication or treatment you would use for each health problem.

**Share your answers.**

1. For which problems would you go to a doctor? use medication? do nothing?

2. What do you do for a sunburn? for a headache?

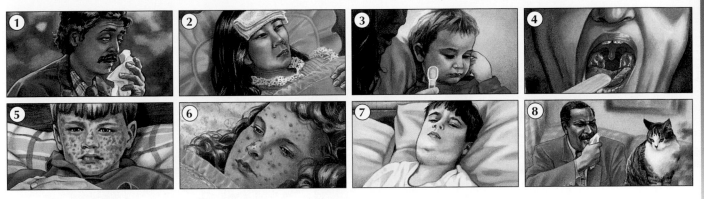

## Common illnesses and childhood diseases

**1.** cold

**2.** flu

**3.** ear infection

**4.** strep throat

**5.** measles

**6.** chicken pox

**7.** mumps

**8.** allergies

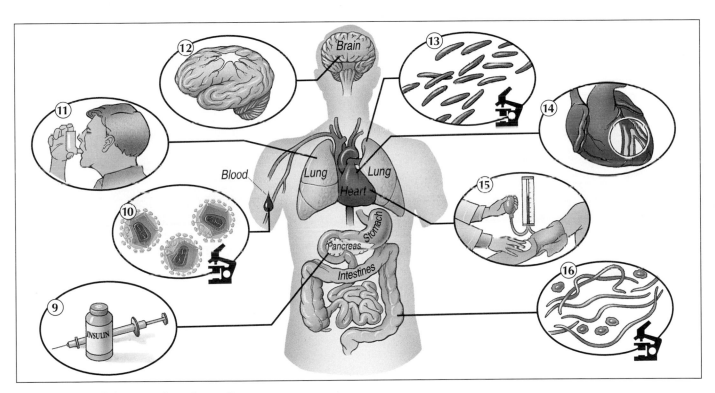

## Medical conditions and serious diseases

**9.** diabetes

**10.** HIV (human immunodeficiency virus)

**11.** asthma

**12.** brain cancer

**13.** TB (tuberculosis)

**14.** heart disease

**15.** high blood pressure

**16.** intestinal parasites

---

**More vocabulary**

**AIDS (acquired immunodeficiency syndrome):** a medical condition that results from contracting the HIV virus

**influenza:** flu

**hypertension:** high blood pressure

**infectious disease:** a disease that is spread through air or water

**Share your answers.**

Which diseases on this page are infectious?

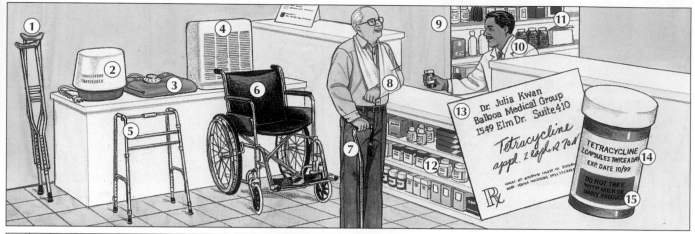

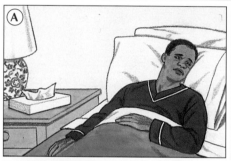

Dr. Julia Kwan
Balboa Medical Group
1549 Elm Dr. Suite 410

Tetracycline
appl. 2 caps x 2 a day

℞

TETRACYCLINE
2 CAPSULES TWICE A DAY
EXP. DATE 10/99

DO NOT TAKE
WITH MILK OR
DAIRY PRODUCTS

| | | |
|---|---|---|
| 1. crutches | 9. pharmacy | A. **Get** bed rest. |
| 2. humidifier | 10. pharmacist | B. **Drink** fluids. |
| 3. heating pad | 11. prescription medication | C. **Change** your diet. |
| 4. air purifier | 12. over-the-counter medication | D. **Exercise.** |
| 5. walker | 13. prescription | E. **Get** an injection. |
| 6. wheelchair | 14. prescription label | F. **Take** medicine. |
| 7. cane | 15. warning label | |
| 8. sling | | |

---

**More vocabulary**

**dosage:** how much medicine you take and how many times a day you take it

**expiration date:** the last day the medicine can be used

**treatment:** something you do to get better

Staying in bed, drinking fluids, and getting physical therapy are treatments.

An injection that stops a person from getting a serious disease is called **an immunization** or **a vaccination.**

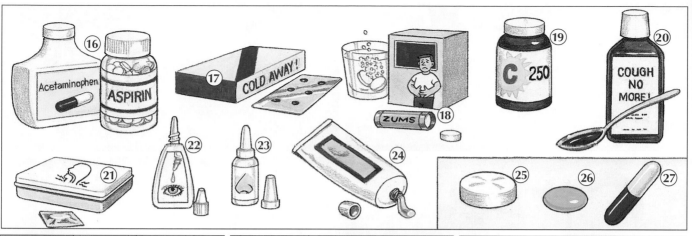

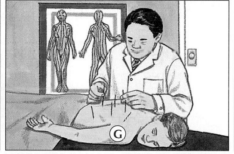

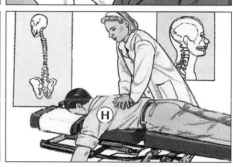

**16.** pain reliever

**17.** cold tablets

**18.** antacid

**19.** vitamins

**20.** cough syrup

**21.** throat lozenges

**22.** eyedrops

**23.** nasal spray

**24.** ointment

**25.** tablet

**26.** pill

**27.** capsule

**28.** orthopedist

**29.** cast

**30.** physical therapist

**31.** brace

**32.** audiologist

**33.** hearing aid

**34.** optometrist

**35.** (eye)glasses

**36.** contact lenses

**G. Get** acupuncture.

**H. Go** to a chiropractor.

**Share your answers.**

**1.** What's the best treatment for a headache? a sore throat? a stomachache? a fever?

**2.** Do you think vitamins are important? Why or why not?

**3.** What treatments are popular in your culture?

# Medical Emergencies

A. **be injured / be hurt**

B. **be** unconscious

C. **be** in shock

D. **have** a heart attack

E. **have** an allergic reaction

F. **get** an electric shock

G. **get** frostbite

H. **burn** (your)self

I. **drown**

J. **swallow** poison

K. **overdose** on drugs

L. **choke**

M. **bleed**

N. **can't breathe**

O. **fall**

P. **break** a bone

**Grammar point:** past tense

| burn | — | burned |
| drown | — | drowned |
| swallow | — | swallowed |
| overdose | — | overdosed |

| choke | — | choked |
| be | — | was, were |
| have | — | had |
| get | — | got |

| bleed | — | bled |
| can't | — | couldn't |
| fall | — | fell |
| break | — | broke |

82

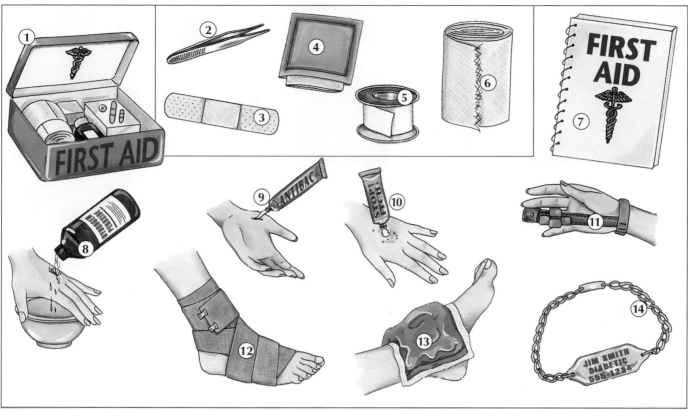

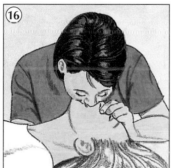

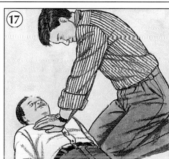

**1.** first aid kit

**2.** tweezers

**3.** adhesive bandage

**4.** sterile pad

**5.** tape

**6.** gauze

**7.** first aid manual

**8.** hydrogen peroxide

**9.** antibacterial ointment

**10.** antihistamine cream

**11.** splint

**12.** elastic bandage

**13.** ice pack

**14.** medical emergency bracelet

**15.** stitches

**16.** rescue breathing

**17.** CPR (cardiopulmonary resuscitation)

**18.** Heimlich maneuver

**Important Note:** Only people who are properly trained should give stitches or do CPR.

**Share your answers.**

**1.** Do you have a First Aid kit in your home? Where can you buy one?

**2.** When do you use hydrogen peroxide? an elastic support bandage? antihistamine cream?

**3.** Do you know first aid? Where did you learn it?

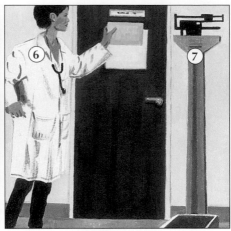

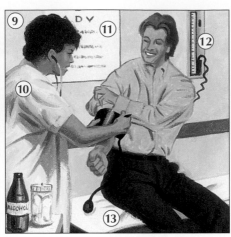

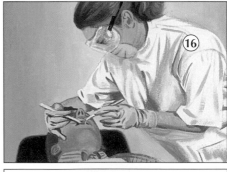

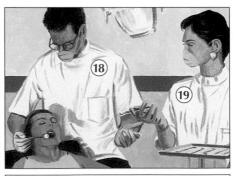

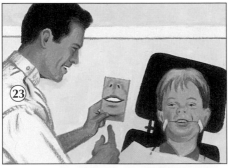

## Medical clinic

1. waiting room
2. receptionist
3. patient
4. insurance card
5. insurance form

6. doctor
7. scale
8. stethoscope
9. examining room
10. nurse

11. eye chart
12. blood pressure gauge
13. examination table
14. syringe
15. thermometer

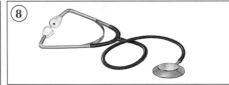

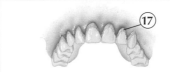

## Dental clinic

16. dental hygienist
17. tartar
18. dentist

19. dental assistant
20. cavity
21. drill

22. filling
23. orthodontist
24. braces

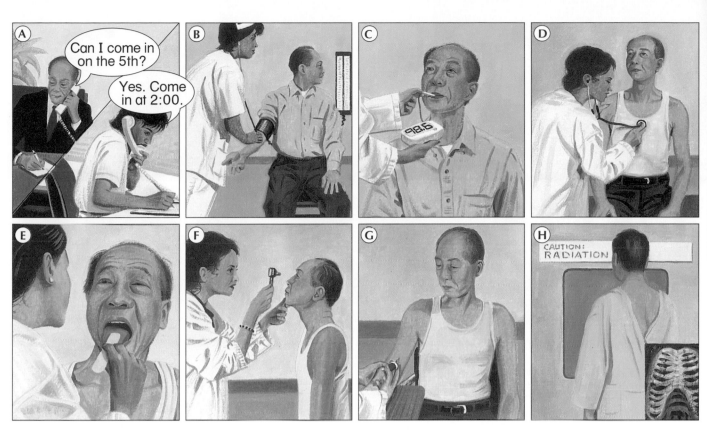

A. **make** an appointment

B. **check**...blood pressure

C. **take**...temperature

D. **listen** to...heart

E. **look** in...throat

F. **examine**...eyes

G. **draw**...blood

H. **get** an X ray

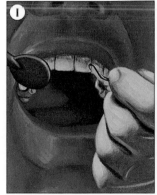
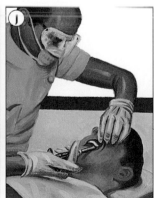
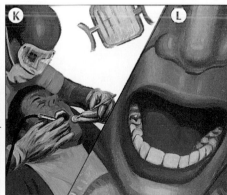
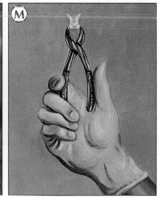

I. **clean**...teeth

J. **give**...a shot of anesthetic

K. **drill** a tooth

L. **fill** a cavity

M. **pull** a tooth

## More vocabulary

**get a checkup:** to go for a medical exam

**extract a tooth:** to pull out a tooth

## Share your answers.

1. What is the average cost of a medical exam in your area?

2. Some people are nervous at the dentist's office. What can they do to relax?

# A Hospital

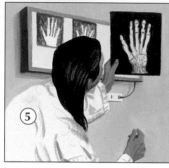

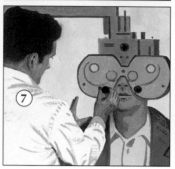

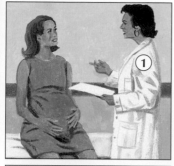
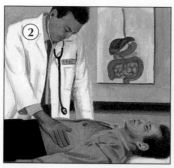
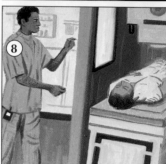

## Hospital staff

1. obstetrician
2. internist
3. cardiologist
4. pediatrician
5. radiologist
6. psychiatrist
7. ophthalmologist
8. X-ray technician

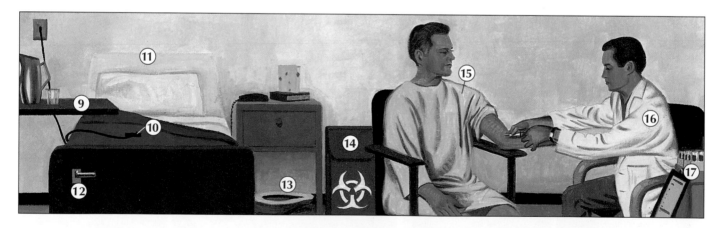

## Patient's room

9. bed table
10. call button
11. hospital bed
12. bed control
13. bedpan
14. medical waste disposal
15. hospital gown
16. lab technician
17. blood work/blood test

## More vocabulary

**nurse practitioner:** a nurse licensed to give medical exams

**specialist:** a doctor who only treats specific medical problems

**gynecologist:** a specialist who examines and treats women

**nurse midwife:** a nurse practitioner who examines pregnant women and delivers babies

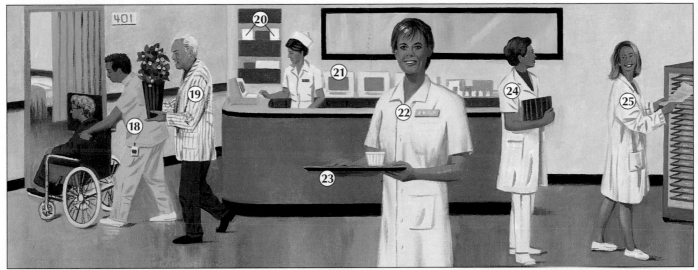

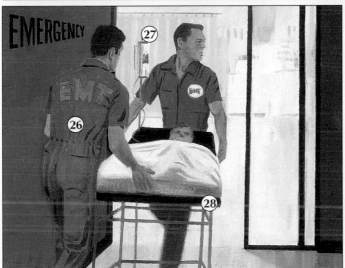

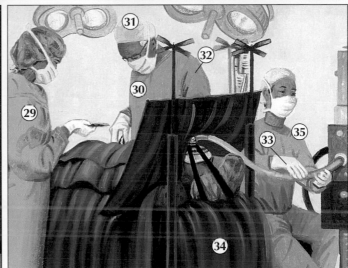

## Nurse's station

**18.** orderly

**19.** volunteer

**20.** medical charts

**21.** vital signs monitor

**22.** RN (registered nurse)

**23.** medication tray

**24.** LPN (licensed practical nurse)/ LVN (licensed vocational nurse)

**25.** dietician

## Emergency room

**26.** emergency medical technician (EMT)

**27.** IV (intravenous drip)

**28.** stretcher/gurney

## Operating room

**29.** surgical nurse

**30.** surgeon

**31.** surgical cap

**32.** surgical gown

**33.** latex gloves

**34.** operating table

**35.** anesthesiologist

---

**Practice asking for the hospital staff.**

*Please get the nurse. I have a question for her.*
*Where's the anesthesiologist? I need to talk to her.*
*I'm looking for the lab technician. Have you seen him?*

**Share your answers.**

1. Have you ever been to an emergency room? Who helped you?

2. Have you ever been in the hospital? How long did you stay?

1. fire station
2. coffee shop
3. bank
4. car dealership
5. hotel

6. church
7. hospital
8. park
9. synagogue
10. theater

11. movie theater
12. gas station
13. furniture store
14. hardware store
15. barber shop

**More vocabulary**

**skyscraper:** a very tall office building

**downtown/city center:** the area in a city with the city hall, courts, and businesses

**Practice giving your destination.**

*I'm going to go <u>downtown</u>.*

*I have to go to <u>the post office</u>.*

| | | |
|---|---|---|
| 16. bakery | 21. health club | 26. parking garage |
| 17. city hall | 22. motel | 27. school |
| 18. courthouse | 23. mosque | 28. library |
| 19. police station | 24. office building | 29. post office |
| 20. market | 25. high-rise building | |

---

**Practice asking for and giving the locations of buildings.**

*Where's the post office?*

   *It's on Oak Street.*

**Share your answers.**

1. Which of the places in this picture do you go to every week?

2. Is it good to live in a city? Why or why not?

3. What famous cities do you know?

| | | |
|---|---|---|
| **1.** Laundromat | **7.** pedestrian | **13.** drive-thru window |
| **2.** drugstore / pharmacy | **8.** crosswalk | **14.** fast food restaurant |
| **3.** convenience store | **9.** street | **15.** bus |
| **4.** photo shop | **10.** curb | **A. cross** the street |
| **5.** parking space | **11.** newsstand | **B. wait** for the light |
| **6.** traffic light | **12.** mailbox | **C. drive** a car |

**More vocabulary**

**neighborhood:** the area close to your home

**do errands:** to make a short trip from your home to buy or pick up something

**Talk about where to buy things.**

*You can buy <u>newspapers</u> at <u>a newsstand</u>.*

*You can buy <u>donuts</u> at <u>a donut shop</u>.*

*You can buy <u>food</u> at <u>a convenience store</u>.*

| | | |
|---|---|---|
| **16.** bus stop | **22.** copy center / print shop | **28.** fire hydrant |
| **17.** corner | **23.** streetlight | **29.** sign |
| **18.** parking meter | **24.** dry cleaners | **30.** street vendor |
| **19.** motorcycle | **25.** nail salon | **31.** cart |
| **20.** donut shop | **26.** sidewalk | **D.** **park** the car |
| **21.** public telephone | **27.** garbage truck | **E.** **ride** a bicycle |

**Share your answers.**

**1.** Do you like to do errands?

**2.** Do you always like to go to the same stores?

**3.** Which businesses in the picture are also in your neighborhood?

**4.** Do you know someone who has a small business? What kind?

**5.** What things can you buy from a street vendor?

| | | |
|---|---|---|
| **1.** music store | **5.** toy store | **9.** travel agency |
| **2.** jewelry store | **6.** pet store | **10.** shoe store |
| **3.** candy store | **7.** card store | **11.** fountain |
| **4.** bookstore | **8.** optician | **12.** florist |

**More vocabulary**

**beauty shop:** hair salon

**men's store:** a store that sells men's clothing

**dress shop:** a store that sells women's clothing

**Talk about where you want to shop in this mall.**

*Let's go to <u>the card store</u>.*

*I need to buy <u>a card</u> for Maggie's birthday.*

13. department store

14. food court

15. video store

16. hair salon

17. maternity shop

18. electronics store

19. directory

20. ice cream stand

21. escalator

22. information booth

**Practice asking for and giving the location of different shops.**

*Where's <u>the maternity shop</u>?*

   *It's on <u>the first floor</u>, next to <u>the hair salon</u>.*

**Share your answers.**

1. Do you like shopping malls? Why or why not?

2. Some people don't go to the mall to shop. Name some other things you can do in a mall.

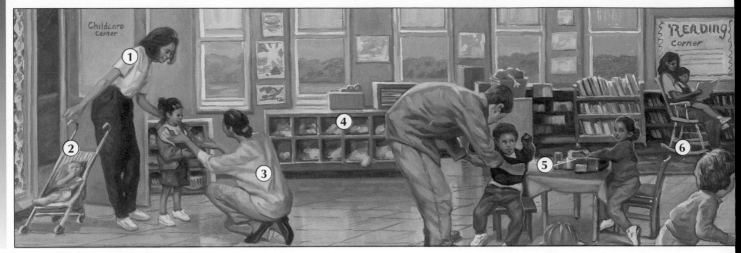

**1.** parent

**3.** childcare worker

**5.** toys

**2.** stroller

**4.** cubby

**6.** rocking chair

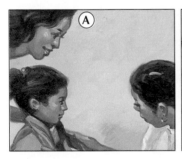

**A. drop off**

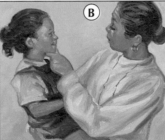

**B. hold**

**C. nurse**

**D. feed**

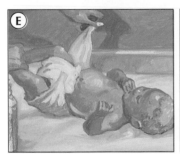

**E. change** diapers

**F. read** a story

**G. pick up**

**H. rock**

**I. tie** shoes

**J. dress**

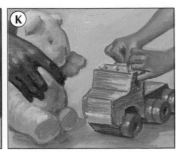

**K. play**

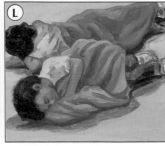

**L. take** a nap

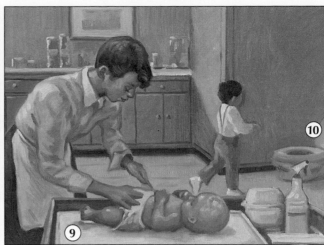

**7.** high chair  **8.** bib  **9.** changing table  **10.** potty seat

| | | |
|---|---|---|
| **11.** playpen | **18.** baby powder | **25.** formula |
| **12.** walker | **19.** disinfectant | **26.** bottle |
| **13.** car safety seat | **20.** disposable diapers | **27.** nipple |
| **14.** baby carrier | **21.** cloth diapers | **28.** baby food |
| **15.** baby backpack | **22.** diaper pins | **29.** pacifier |
| **16.** carriage | **23.** diaper pail | **30.** teething ring |
| **17.** wipes | **24.** training pants | **31.** rattle |

1. envelope

2. letter

3. postcard

4. greeting card

5. package

6. letter carrier

7. return address

8. mailing address

9. postmark

10. stamp/postage

11. certified mail

12. priority mail

13. air letter/aerogramme

14. ground post/ parcel post

15. Express Mail/ overnight mail

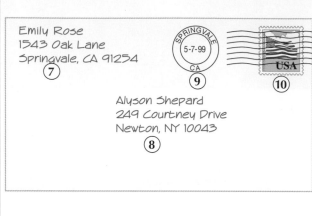

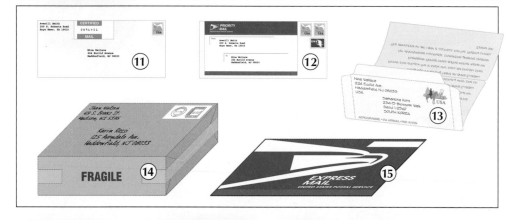

Emily Rose
1543 Oak Lane
Springvale, CA 91254
**7**

SPRINGVALE
5-7-99
CA
**9**

USA
**10**

Alyson Shepard
249 Courtney Drive
Newton, NY 10043
**8**

FRAGILE **14**

EXPRESS MAIL
UNITED STATES POSTAL SERVICE **15**

A. **address** a postcard

B. **send** it/**mail** it

C. **deliver** it

D. **receive** it

1. teller

2. vault

3. ATM (automated teller machine)

4. security guard

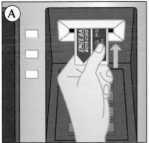

5. passbook

6. savings account number

7. checkbook

8. checking account number

9. ATM card

10. monthly statement

11. balance

12. deposit slip

13. safe-deposit box

## Using the ATM machine

A. **Insert** your ATM card.

B. **Enter** your PIN number.*

C. **Make** a deposit.

D. **Withdraw** cash.

E. **Transfer** funds.

F. **Remove** your ATM card.

*PIN: personal identification number

## More vocabulary

**overdrawn account:** When there is not enough money in an account to pay a check, we say the account is overdrawn.

## Share your answers.

1. Do you use a bank?

2. Do you use an ATM card?

3. Name some things you can put in a safe-deposit box.

1. reference librarian
2. reference desk
3. atlas
4. microfilm reader
5. microfilm
6. periodical section

7. magazine
8. newspaper
9. online catalog
10. card catalog
11. media section
12. audiocassette

13. videocassette
14. CD (compact disc)
15. record
16. checkout desk
17. library clerk
18. encyclopedia

19. library card
20. library book
21. title
22. author

**More vocabulary**

**check a book out:** to borrow a book from the library

**nonfiction:** real information, history or true stories

**fiction:** stories from the author's imagination

**Share your answers.**

1. Do you have a library card?
2. Do you prefer to buy books or borrow them from the library?

"You have the right to remain silent…"

"Bail is set at $20,000."

**A. arrest** a suspect

**B. hire** a lawyer / **hire** an attorney

**C. appear** in court

1. police officer

3. guard

5. defendant

2. handcuffs

4. defense attorney

6. judge

**D. stand trial**

8. jury

10. prosecuting attorney

12. court reporter

7. courtroom

9. evidence

11. witness

13. bailiff

Guilty

7 years

**E. give** the verdict*

**F. sentence** the defendant

**G. go** to jail / **go** to prison

**H. be released**

14. convict

*Note: There are two possible verdicts, "guilty" and "not guilty."

## Share your answers.

1. What are some differences between the legal system in the United States and the one in your country?

2. Do you want to be on a jury? Why or why not?

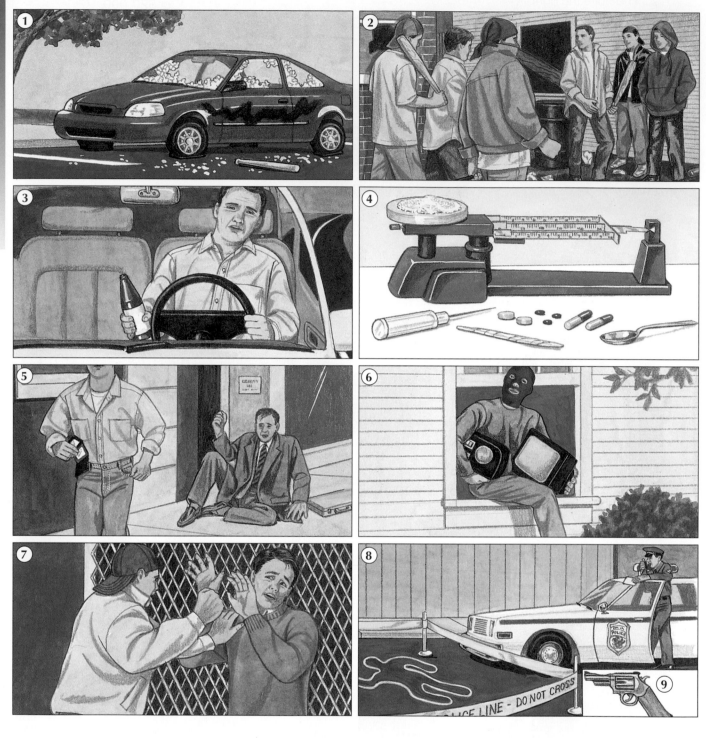

1. vandalism

2. gang violence

3. drunk driving

4. illegal drugs

5. mugging

6. burglary

7. assault

8. murder

9. gun

**More vocabulary**

**commit a crime:** to do something illegal

**criminal:** someone who commits a crime

**victim:** someone who is hurt or killed by someone else

**Share your answers.**

1. Is there too much crime on TV? in the movies?

2. Do you think people become criminals from watching crime on TV?

**A.** **Walk** with a friend.

**B.** **Stay** on well-lit streets.

**C.** **Hold** your purse close to your body.

**D.** **Protect** your wallet.

**E.** **Lock** your doors.

**F.** **Don't open** your door to strangers.

**G.** **Don't drink** and **drive**.

**H.** **Report** crimes to the police.

## More vocabulary

**Neighborhood Watch**: a group of neighbors who watch for criminals in their neighborhood

**designated drivers**: people who don't drink alcoholic beverages so that they can drive drinkers home

## Share your answers.

1. Do you feel safe in your neighborhood?
2. Look at the pictures. Which of these things do you do?
3. What other things do you do to stay safe?

# Emergencies and Natural Disasters

1. lost child
2. car accident
3. airplane crash

4. explosion
5. earthquake
6. mudslide

7. fire
8. firefighter
9. fire truck

**Practice reporting a fire.**

*This is <u>Lisa Broad</u>. There is a fire.*
*The address is <u>323 Oak Street.</u>*
*Please send someone quickly.*

**Share your answers.**

1. Can you give directions to your home if there is a fire?

2. What information do you give to the other driver if you are in a car accident?

**10.** drought

**11.** blizzard

**12.** hurricane

**13.** tornado

**14.** volcanic eruption

**15.** tidal wave

**16.** flood

**17.** search and rescue team

## Share your answers.

**1.** Which disasters are common in your area? Which never happen?

**2.** What can you do to prepare for emergencies?

**3.** Do you have emergency numbers near your telephone?

**4.** What organizations will help you in an emergency?

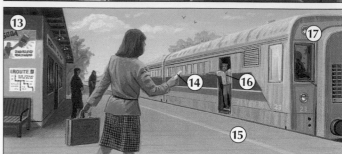

| | | | |
|---|---|---|---|
| **1.** bus stop | **7.** passenger | **13.** train station | **19.** taxi stand |
| **2.** route | **8.** bus driver | **14.** ticket | **20.** taxi driver |
| **3.** schedule | **9.** subway | **15.** platform | **21.** meter |
| **4.** bus | **10.** track | **16.** conductor | **22.** taxi license |
| **5.** fare | **11.** token | **17.** train | **23.** ferry |
| **6.** transfer | **12.** fare card | **18.** taxi / cab | |

**More vocabulary**

**hail a taxi:** to get a taxi driver's attention by raising your hand

**miss the bus:** to arrive at the bus stop late

**Talk about how you and your friends come to school.**

*I take the bus to school.*　　*He drives to school.*
*You take the train.*　　　*She walks to school.*
*We take the subway.*　　　*They ride bikes.*

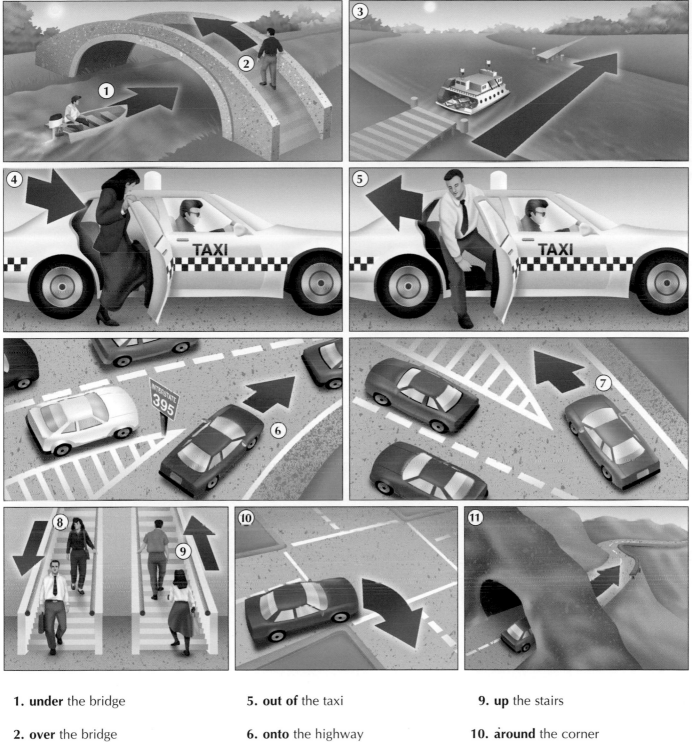

1. **under** the bridge

2. **over** the bridge

3. **across** the water

4. **into** the taxi

5. **out of** the taxi

6. **onto** the highway

7. **off** the highway

8. **down** the stairs

9. **up** the stairs

10. **around** the corner

11. **through** the tunnel

**Grammar point:** *into, out of, on, off*

We say, *get **into** a taxi or a car.*
But we say, *get **on** a bus, a train, or a plane.*

We say, *get **out of** a taxi or a car.*
But we say, *get **off** a bus, a train, or a plane.*

# Cars and Trucks

1. subcompact
2. compact
3. midsize car
4. full-size car
5. convertible

6. sports car
7. pickup truck
8. station wagon
9. SUV (sports utility vehicle)

10. minivan
11. camper
12. dump truck
13. tow truck
14. moving van

15. tractor trailer/semi
16. cab
17. trailer

## More vocabulary

**make:** the name of the company that makes the car

**model:** the style of car

## Share your answers.

1. What is your favorite kind of car?

2. What kind of car is good for a big family? for a single person?

## Directions

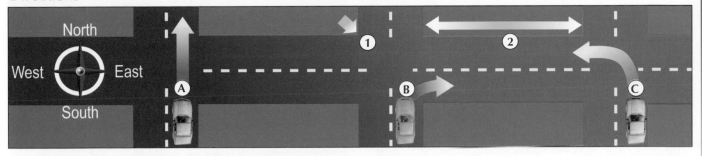

North
West · East
South

A. go straight

B. turn right

C. turn left

1. corner

2. block

## Signs

3. stop

4. do not enter/wrong way

5. speed limit

6. one way

7. U-turn OK

8. no outlet/dead end

9. right turn only

10. pedestrian crossing

11. railroad crossing

12. no parking

13. school crossing

14. handicapped parking

**More vocabulary**

**right-of-way:** the right to go first

**yield:** to give another person or car the right-of-way

**Share your answers.**

1. Which traffic signs are the same in your country?

2. Do pedestrians have the right-of-way in your city?

3. What is the speed limit in front of your school? your home?

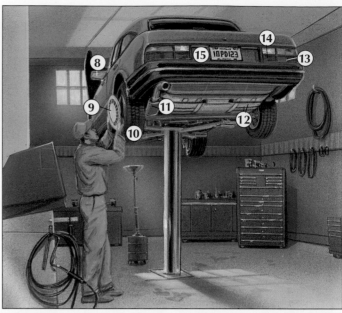

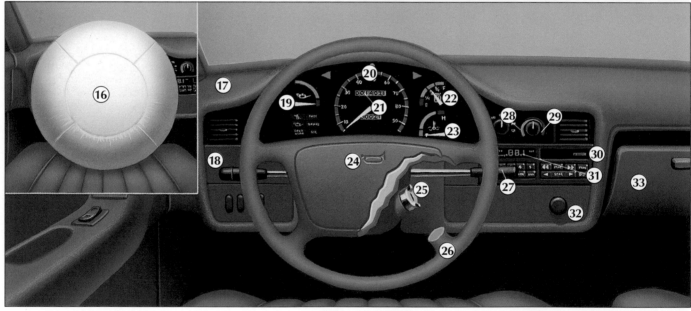

| | | | |
|---|---|---|---|
| **1.** rearview mirror | **10.** tire | **19.** oil gauge | **28.** air conditioning |
| **2.** windshield | **11.** muffler | **20.** speedometer | **29.** heater |
| **3.** windshield wipers | **12.** gas tank | **21.** odometer | **30.** tape deck |
| **4.** turn signal | **13.** brake light | **22.** gas gauge | **31.** radio |
| **5.** headlight | **14.** taillight | **23.** temperature gauge | **32.** cigarette lighter |
| **6.** hood | **15.** license plate | **24.** horn | **33.** glove compartment |
| **7.** bumper | **16.** air bag | **25.** ignition | |
| **8.** sideview mirror | **17.** dashboard | **26.** steering wheel | |
| **9.** hubcap | **18.** turn signal | **27.** gearshift | |

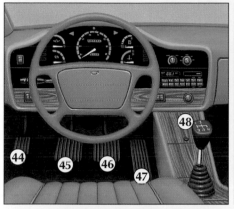

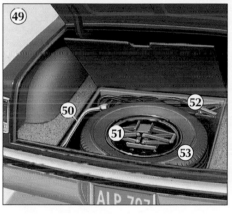

**34.** lock

**35.** front seat

**36.** seat belt

**37.** shoulder harness

**38.** backseat

**39.** child safety seat

**40.** fuel injection system

**41.** engine

**42.** radiator

**43.** battery

**44.** emergency brake

**45.** clutch*

**46.** brake pedal

**47.** accelerator/gas pedal

**48.** stick shift

**49.** trunk

**50.** lug wrench

**51.** jack

**52.** jumper cables

**53.** spare tire

**54.** The car needs **gas**.

**55.** The car needs **oil**.

**56.** The radiator needs **coolant**.

**57.** The car needs **a smog check**.

**58.** The battery needs **recharging**.

**59.** The tires need **air**.

**\*Note:** Standard transmission cars have a clutch; automatic transmission cars do not.

1. airline terminal
2. airline representative
3. check-in counter
4. arrival and departure monitors
5. gate
6. boarding area
7. control tower
8. helicopter

9. airplane
10. overhead compartment
11. cockpit
12. pilot
13. flight attendant
14. oxygen mask
15. airsickness bag
16. tray table

17. baggage claim area
18. carousel
19. luggage carrier
20. customs
21. customs officer
22. declaration form
23. passenger

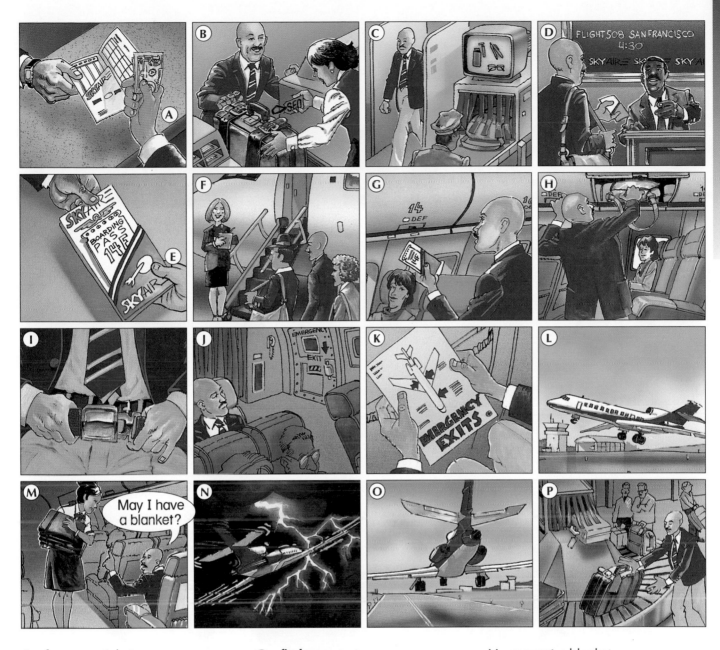

A. **buy** your ticket

B. **check** your bags

C. **go through** security

D. **check in** at the gate

E. **get** your boarding pass

F. **board** the plane

G. **find** your seat

H. **stow** your carry-on bag

I. **fasten** your seat belt

J. **look for** the emergency exit

K. **look at** the emergency card

L. **take off / leave**

M. **request** a blanket

N. **experience** turbulence

O. **land / arrive**

P. **claim** your baggage

**More vocabulary**

**destination:** the place the passenger is going

**departure time:** the time the plane takes off

**arrival time:** the time the plane lands

**direct flight:** a plane trip between two cities with no stops

**stopover:** a stop before reaching the destination, sometimes to change planes

# Types of Schools

**1.** public school

**2.** private school

**3.** parochial school

**4.** preschool

**5.** elementary school

**6.** middle school/
junior high school

**7.** high school

**8.** adult school

**9.** vocational school/trade school

**10.** college/university

**Note:** In the U.S. most children begin school at age 5 (in kindergarten) and graduate from high school at 17 or 18.

## More vocabulary

When students graduate from a college or university they receive a **degree:**

Bachelor's degree—usually 4 years of study

Master's degree—an additional 1–3 years of study

Doctorate—an additional 3–5 years of study

**community college:** a two-year college where students can get an Associate of Arts degree.

**graduate school:** a school in a university where students study for their master's and doctorates.

**1.** writing assignment

**B. Edit** your paper.

**D. Rewrite** your paper.

**2.** paper / composition

**A. Write** a first draft.

**C. Get** feedback.

**E. Turn in** your paper.

③ My life in the U.S.

④ I arrived in this country in 1996. My family did not come with me. I was homesick, nervous, and a little excited. I had no job and no friends here. I lived with my aunt and my daily routine ⑤ was always the same: get up, look for a job, go to bed. At night I remembered my mother's words to me, "Son, you can always come home!" I was homesick and scared, but I did not go home.

I started to study English at night. English is a difficult language and many times I was too tired to study. One teacher, Mrs. Armstrong, was very kind to me. She showed me many

**3.** title

**4.** sentence

**5.** paragraph

## Punctuation

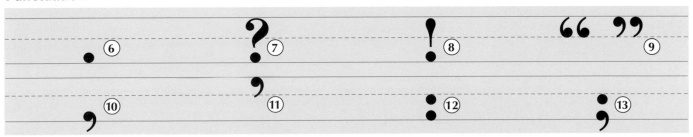

**6.** period

**9.** quotation marks

**12.** colon

**7.** question mark

**10.** comma

**13.** semicolon

**8.** exclamation mark

**11.** apostrophe

Exploration

War

Immigration

| **Historical and Political Events** | **1492 →** French, Spanish, English explorers | **1607–1750** Colonies along Atlantic coast founded by Northern Europeans | **1619** 1st African slave sold in Virginia |
| | | | **1653** 1st Indian reservation in Virginia |

**Before 1700**                                                    **1700**

| **Immigration*** | **1607** 1st English in Virginia | **1610** Spanish at Santa Fe | |

| **Population**** | Before 1700: Native American: 1,000,000+ | | 1700: colonists: 250,000 |

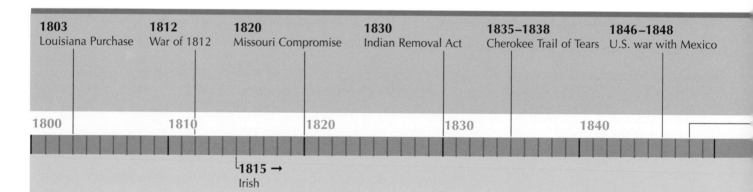

| **1803** Louisiana Purchase | **1812** War of 1812 | **1820** Missouri Compromise | **1830** Indian Removal Act | **1835–1838** Cherokee Trail of Tears | **1846–1848** U.S. war with Mexico |

1800          1810          1820          1830          1840

**1815 →**
Irish

1800: citizens and free blacks: 5,300,000          slaves: 450,000

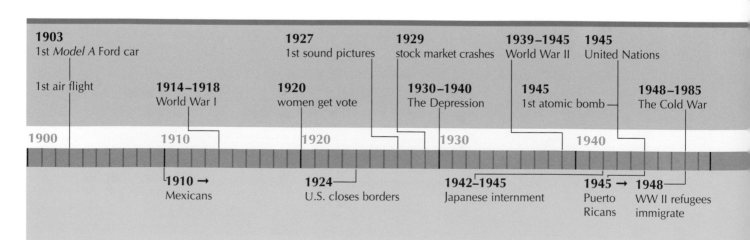

| **1903** 1st *Model A* Ford car | **1927** 1st sound pictures | **1929** stock market crashes | **1939–1945** World War II | **1945** United Nations |

1st air flight

| **1914–1918** World War I | **1920** women get vote | **1930–1940** The Depression | **1945** 1st atomic bomb | **1948–1985** The Cold War |

1900          1910          1920          1930          1940

**1910 →**
Mexicans

**1924**
U.S. closes borders

**1942–1945**
Japanese internment

**1945 →**
Puerto Ricans

**1948**
WW II refugees immigrate

1900: 75,994,000

*Immigration dates indicate a time when large numbers of that group first began to immigrate to the U.S.
**All population figures before 1790 are estimates. Figures after 1790 are based on the official U.S. census.

Movement

Election

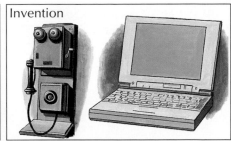

Invention

**1754–1763**
French and Indian War

**1775–1783**
Revolutionary War

**1776**
Declaration of
Independence

**1788**
U.S. Constitution

**1791**
Bill of Rights

**1789** Washington 1st President

1750        1760        1770        1780        1790

**1750 →**
Scots, Irish, Germans

**1790 →**
Haitians

1750: Native American: 1,000,000 +        colonists and free blacks: 1,171,000        slaves: 200,000

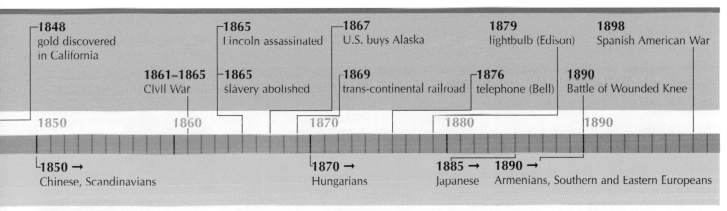

**1848**
gold discovered
in California

**1865**
Lincoln assassinated

**1867**
U.S. buys Alaska

**1879**
lightbulb (Edison)

**1898**
Spanish American War

**1861–1865**
Civil War

**1865**
slavery abolished

**1869**
trans-continental railroad

**1876**
telephone (Bell)

**1890**
Battle of Wounded Knee

1850        1860        1870        1880        1890

**1850 →**
Chinese, Scandinavians

**1870 →**
Hungarians

**1885 →**
Japanese

**1890 →**
Armenians, Southern and Eastern Europeans

1850: 23,191,000

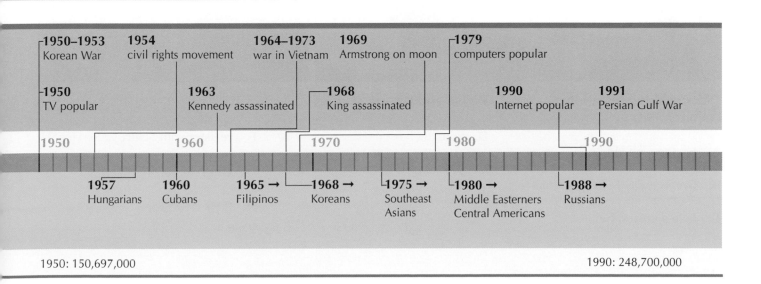

**1950–1953**
Korean War

**1954**
civil rights movement

**1964–1973**
war in Vietnam

**1969**
Armstrong on moon

**1979**
computers popular

**1950**
TV popular

**1963**
Kennedy assassinated

**1968**
King assassinated

**1990**
Internet popular

**1991**
Persian Gulf War

1950        1960        1970        1980        1990

**1957**
Hungarians

**1960**
Cubans

**1965 →**
Filipinos

**1968 →**
Koreans

**1975 →**
Southeast
Asians

**1980 →**
Middle Easterners
Central Americans

**1988 →**
Russians

1950: 150,697,000        1990: 248,700,000

## BRANCHES OF GOVERNMENT

Legislative

Executive

Judicial

1. The House of Representatives
2. congresswoman/congressman
3. The Senate
4. senator

5. The White House
6. president
7. vice president

8. The Supreme Court
9. chief justice
10. justices

## Citizenship application requirements

A. **be** 18 years old

B. **live** in the U.S. for five years

C. **take** a citizenship test

## Rights and responsibilities

D. **vote**

E. **pay** taxes

F. **register** with Selective Service*

G. **serve** on a jury

H. **obey** the law

*Note: All males 18 to 26 who live in the U.S. are required to register with Selective Service.

| | |
|---|---|
| **1.** rain forest | **7.** peninsula |
| **2.** waterfall | **8.** island |
| **3.** river | **9.** bay |
| **4.** desert | **10.** beach |
| **5.** sand dune | **11.** forest |
| **6.** ocean | **12.** shore |

| | |
|---|---|
| **13.** lake | **19.** plains |
| **14.** mountain peak | **20.** meadow |
| **15.** mountain range | **21.** pond |
| **16.** hills | |
| **17.** canyon | |
| **18.** valley | |

**More vocabulary**

**a body of water:** a river, lake, or ocean
**stream/creek:** a very small river

**Talk about where you live and where you like to go.**

*I live in <u>a valley</u>. There is <u>a lake</u> <u>nearby</u>.*
*I like to go to <u>the beach</u>.*

# Mathematics

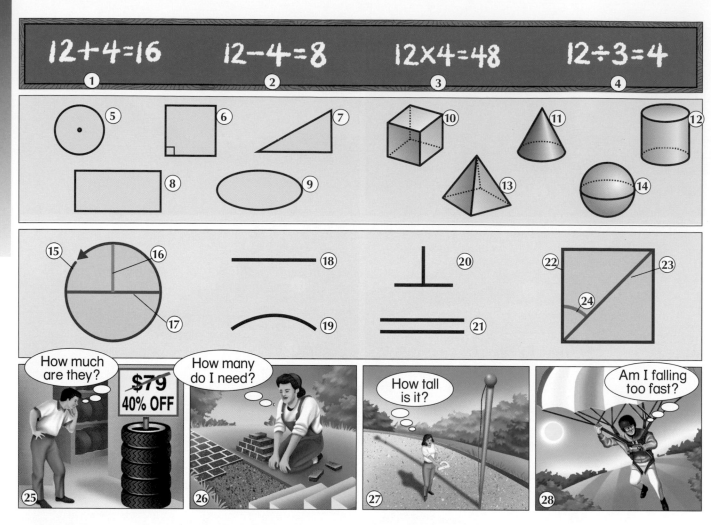

## Operations

**1.** addition

**2.** subtraction

**3.** multiplication

**4.** division

## Shapes

**5.** circle

**6.** square

**7.** triangle

**8.** rectangle

**9.** oval/ellipse

## Solids

**10.** cube

**11.** cone

**12.** cylinder

**13.** pyramid

**14.** sphere

## Parts of a circle

**15.** circumference

**16.** radius

**17.** diameter

## Lines

**18.** straight

**19.** curved

**20.** perpendicular

**21.** parallel

## Parts of a square

**22.** side

**23.** diagonal

**24.** angle

## Types of math

**25.** algebra

**26.** geometry

**27.** trigonometry

**28.** calculus

## More vocabulary

**total:** the answer to an addition problem

**difference:** the answer to a subtraction problem

**product:** the answer to a multiplication problem

**quotient:** the answer to a division problem

**pi (π):** the number when you divide the circumference of a circle by its diameter (approximately = 3.14)

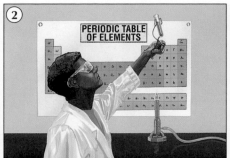

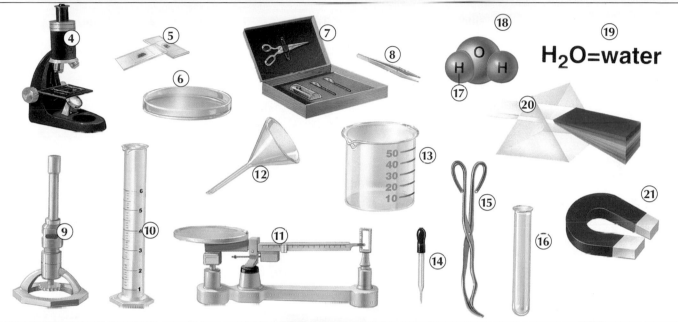

H₂O=water

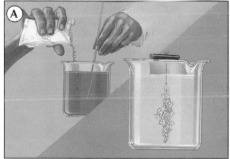

1. biology

2. chemistry

3. physics

4. microscope

5. slide

6. petri dish

7. dissection kit

8. forceps

9. Bunsen burner

10. graduated cylinder

11. balance

12. funnel

13. beaker

14. dropper

15. crucible tongs

16. test tube

17. atom

18. molecule

19. formula

20. prism

21. magnet

A. **do** an experiment

B. **observe**

C. **record** results

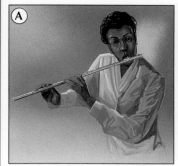

**A. play** an instrument

**B. sing** a song

**1.** orchestra

**2.** rock band

## Woodwinds

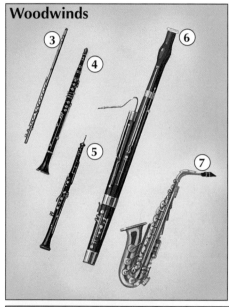

## Strings

## Brass

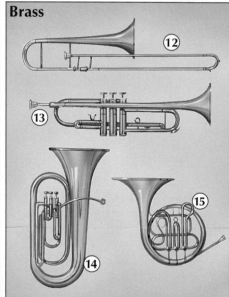

## Percussion

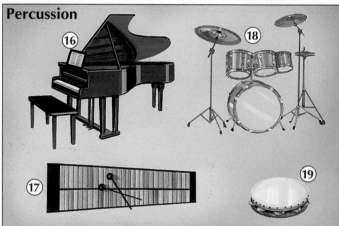

## Other Instruments

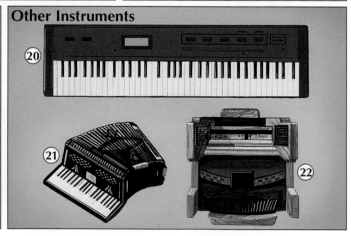

| | | | |
|---|---|---|---|
| **3.** flute | **8.** violin | **13.** trumpet/horn | **18.** drums |
| **4.** clarinet | **9.** cello | **14.** tuba | **19.** tambourine |
| **5.** oboe | **10.** bass | **15.** French horn | **20.** electric keyboard |
| **6.** bassoon | **11.** guitar | **16.** piano | **21.** accordion |
| **7.** saxophone | **12.** trombone | **17.** xylophone | **22.** organ |

It's a chair.

C'est une chaise.

**1.** art

**2.** business education

**3.** chorus

**4.** computer science

**5.** driver's education

**6.** economics

**7.** English as a second language

**8.** foreign language

**9.** home economics

**10.** industrial arts/shop

**11.** PE (physical education)

**12.** theater arts

**More vocabulary**

**core course:** a subject students have to take

**elective:** a subject students choose to take

**Share your answers.**

**1.** What are your favorite subjects?

**2.** In your opinion, what subjects are most important? Why?

**3.** What foreign languages are taught in your school?

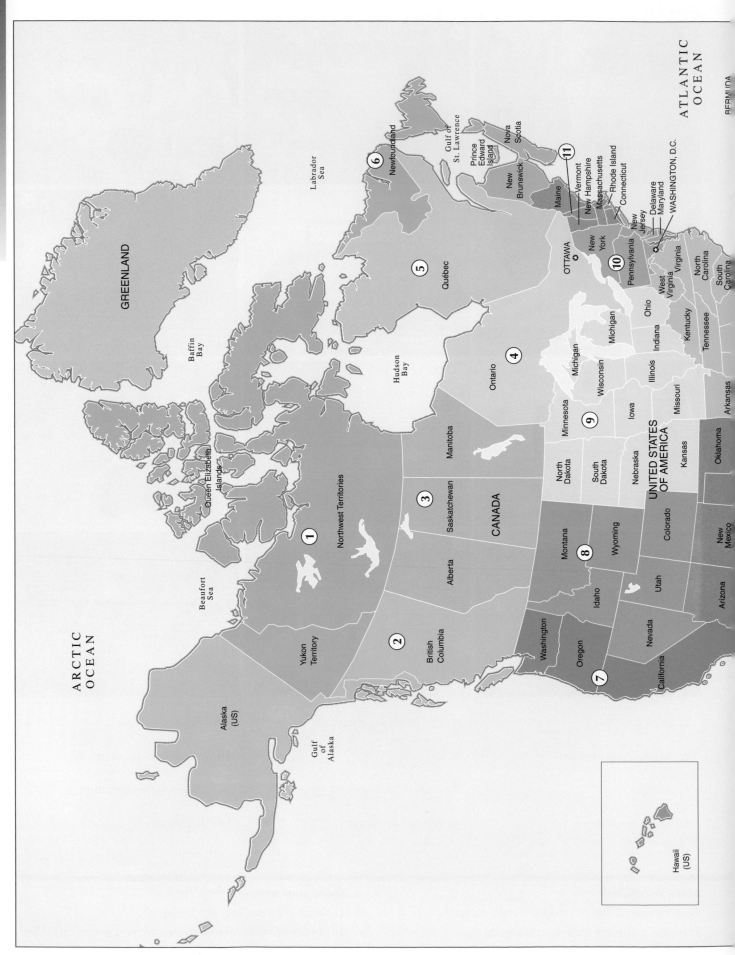

ATLANTIC OCEAN

BERMUDA

Gulf of St. Lawrence

Newfoundland

Labrador Sea

Prince Edward Island

Nova Scotia

New Brunswick

Maine

Vermont

New Hampshire

Massachusetts

Rhode Island

Connecticut

New Jersey

Delaware

Maryland

WASHINGTON, D.C.

New York

Pennsylvania

West Virginia

Virginia

North Carolina

South Carolina

OTTAWA

Québec

GREENLAND

Baffin Bay

Hudson Bay

Ontario

Michigan

Michigan

Ohio

Indiana

Kentucky

Tennessee

Illinois

Missouri

Arkansas

Wisconsin

Iowa

Minnesota

North Dakota

South Dakota

Nebraska

Kansas

Oklahoma

UNITED STATES OF AMERICA

Queen Elizabeth Islands

Northwest Territories

Manitoba

Saskatchewan

CANADA

Alberta

British Columbia

Montana

Wyoming

Colorado

New Mexico

Idaho

Utah

Nevada

Arizona

Washington

Oregon

California

Yukon Territory

Beaufort Sea

ARCTIC OCEAN

Alaska (US)

Gulf of Alaska

Hawaii (US)

# North America and Central America

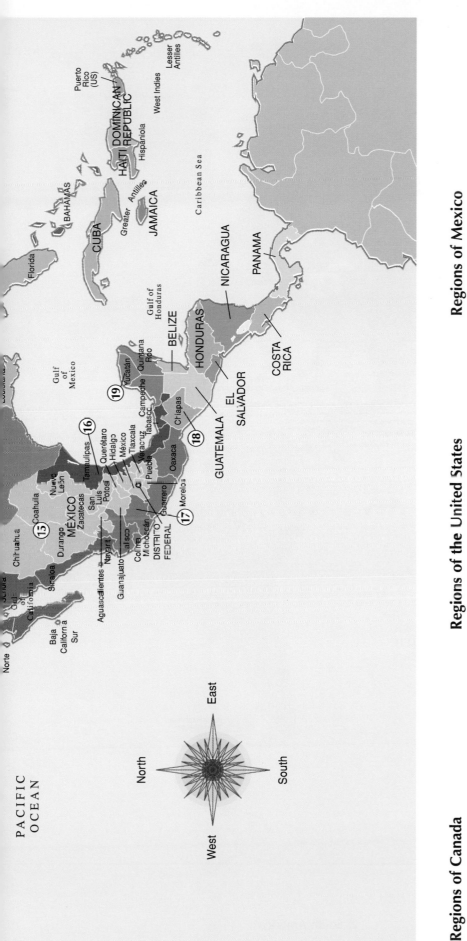

## Regions of Canada

1. Northern Canada

2. British Columbia

3. The Prairie Provinces

4. Ontario

5. Québec

6. The Atlantic Provinces

## Regions of the United States

7. The Pacific States/the West Coast

8. The Rocky Mountain States

9. The Midwest

10. The Mid-Atlantic States

11. New England

12. The Southwest

13. The Southeast/the South

## Regions of Mexico

14. The Pacific Northwest

15. The Plateau of Mexico

16. The Gulf Coastal Plain

17. The Southern Uplands

18. The Chiapas Highlands

19. The Yucatan Peninsula

123

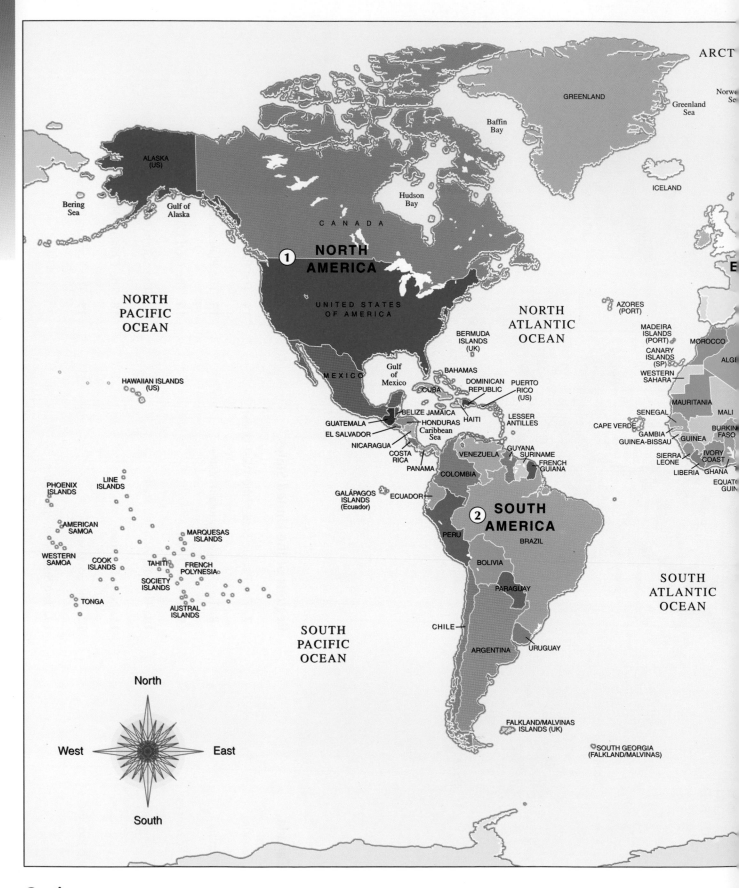

ARCT

GREENLAND

Greenland
Sea

Norwe
Se

Baffin
Bay

ICELAND

ALASKA
(US)

Bering
Sea

Gulf of
Alaska

Hudson
Bay

C A N A D A

① **NORTH
AMERICA**

NORTH
PACIFIC
OCEAN

UNITED STATES
OF AMERICA

NORTH
ATLANTIC
OCEAN

AZORES
(PORT)

MADEIRA
ISLANDS
(PORT)

MOROCCO

CANARY
ISLANDS
(SP)

ALGE

WESTERN
SAHARA

BERMUDA
ISLANDS
(UK)

MEXICO

Gulf
of
Mexico

BAHAMAS

DOMINICAN
REPUBLIC

PUERTO
RICO
(US)

CUBA

HAWAIIAN ISLANDS
(US)

MAURITANIA

SENEGAL

MALI

CAPE VERDE

BURKIN
FASO

GUATEMALA
EL SALVADOR

BELIZE JAMAICA
HONDURAS

HAITI

LESSER
ANTILLES

GAMBIA
GUINEA-BISSAU

GUINEA

NICARAGUA

Caribbean
Sea

SIERRA
LEONE

IVORY
COAST

COSTA
RICA

PANAMA

GUYANA
SURINAME
FRENCH
GUIANA

VENEZUELA

LIBERIA

GHANA

COLOMBIA

EQUATO
GUIN

PHOENIX
ISLANDS

LINE
ISLANDS

GALÁPAGOS
ISLANDS
(Ecuador)

ECUADOR

② **SOUTH
AMERICA**

PERU

BRAZIL

SOUTH
ATLANTIC
OCEAN

AMERICAN
SAMOA

MARQUESAS
ISLANDS

BOLIVIA

WESTERN
SAMOA

COOK
ISLANDS

TAHITI

FRENCH
POLYNESIA

PARAGUAY

SOCIETY
ISLANDS

TONGA

AUSTRAL
ISLANDS

CHILE

URUGUAY

SOUTH
PACIFIC
OCEAN

ARGENTINA

North

West

East

FALKLAND/MALVINAS
ISLANDS (UK)

SOUTH GEORGIA
(FALKLAND/MALVINAS)

South

## Continents

**1.** North America

**2.** South America

CEAN

SVALBARD
(NORWAY)

FRANZ JOSEF LAND
(RUSSIA)

Barents Sea

R U S S I A

④ ASIA

③

E

Black Sea

KAZAKHSTAN

Caspian
Sea

MONGOLIA

Sea of
Okhotsk

Bering
Sea

ALEUTIAN ISLANDS
(US)

GEORGIA
AZERBAIJAN
ARMENIA
TURKEY
SYRIA
CYPRUS
LEBANON
Mediterranean Sea
ISRAEL
JORDAN
LIBYA
EGYPT

UZBEKISTAN KYRGYZSTAN
TURKMENISTAN
TAJIKISTAN

NORTH
KOREA
SOUTH
KOREA

Sea of
Japan

JAPAN

NORTH
PACIFIC
OCEAN

IRAQ
KUWAIT
BAHRAIN
SAUDI
ARABIA
Red
Sea

AFGHANISTAN
IRAN
Persian
Gulf
QATAR
UNITED
ARAB
EMIRATES
OMAN

PAKISTAN

CHINA

East
China
Sea

TAIWAN

VOLCANO
ISLANDS

DAITO
ISLANDS
(JAPAN)
PARECE
VELA
(JAPAN)

WAKE ISLAND
(US)

NORTHERN
MARIANA
ISLANDS
(US)

⑤

NEPAL
BHUTAN
INDIA
BANGLADESH

Arabian
Sea

MYANMAR
LAOS

HONG
KONG

Philippine
Sea

GUAM
(US)

MARSHALL
ISLANDS

FRICA

CHAD
SUDAN

CENTRAL
AFRICAN
REPUBLIC
ENOON

ERITREA
DJIBOUTI
ETHIOPIA

YEMEN
SOMALIA

SOCOTRA
(YEMEN)

ANDAMAN
ISLANDS
(INDIA)

THAILAND
CAMDODIA

NICOBAR
ISLANDS
(INDIA)

VIETNAM
PHILIPPINES

South
China
Sea

BRUNEI

YAP
ISLANDS

PALAU

FEDERATED STATE
OF MICRONESIA

NAURU
KIRIBATI

UGANDA
KENYA

ONGO
DEMOCRATIC
REPUBLIC
OF THE
CONGO
TANZANIA

RWANDA
BURUNDI

ZANZIBAR

MALDIVE
ISLANDS

SRI
LANKA

MALAYSIA
SINGAPORE
SUMATRA
BORNEO
CELEBES

JAVA

NEW GUINEA
PAPUA
NEW
GUINEA

SOLOMON
ISLANDS

TUVALU

ANGOLA
ZAMBIA MALAWI
MOZAMBIQUE
ZIMBABWE
NAMIBIA
BOTSWANA

SEYCHELLES
COMOROS

CHAGOS ARCHIPELAGO

INDONESIA

INDIAN
OCEAN

Coral
Sea

VANUATU

MADAGASCAR
MAURITIUS

CORAL SEA
ISLANDS
TERRITORY
(AUSTRALIA)

FIJI

SWAZILAND

LESOTHO
SOUTH
AFRICA

⑥ AUSTRALIA

NEW
CALEDONIA

SOUTH
PACIFIC
OCEAN

ICELAND

NORWAY

FINLAND

SWEDEN

North
Sea

Baltic
Sea

ESTONIA

RUSSIA

TASMANIA
(AUSTRALIA)

NORTH
ISLAND

NEW
ZEALAND

SOUTH
ISLAND

DENMARK
NETHER-
LANDS
IRELAND
UNITED
KINGDOM

LATVIA
LITHUANIA
RUSSIA

BELARUS

GERMANY

BELGIUM
LUXEMBOURG
LIECHTENSTEIN
SWITZER-
LAND
FRANCE

POLAND

CZECH
REPUBLIC
AUSTRIA
SLOVENIA
SLOVAKIA
HUNGARY
CROATIA

UKRAINE

MOLDOVA

ROMANIA

BOSNIA
HERZEGOVINA
MONTENEGRO

SERBIA

SOUTHERN
OCEAN

ANDORRA
MONACO
SPAIN
PORTUGAL
BALEARIC
ISLANDS
(SP)

CORSICA
(FR)

SARDINIA
(IT)

ITALY
ALBANIA

BULGARIA
MACEDONIA

Black Sea

GREECE

SICILY (IT)

MALTA
CRETE

CYPRUS

Mediterranean Sea

**ANTARCTICA** ⑦

**3.** Europe

**4.** Asia

**5.** Africa

**6.** Australia

**7.** Antarctica

# Energy and the Environment

## Energy resources

**1.** solar energy

**2.** wind

**3.** natural gas

**4.** coal

**5.** hydroelectric power

**6.** oil/petroleum

**7.** geothermal energy

**8.** nuclear energy

## Pollution

**9.** hazardous waste

**10.** air pollution/smog

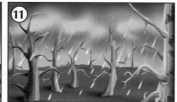
**11.** acid rain

**12.** water pollution

**13.** radiation

**14.** pesticide poisoning

**15.** oil spill

## Conservation

**A.** **recycle**

**B.** **save** water/**conserve** water

**C.** **save** energy/**conserve** energy

---

**Share your answers.**

1. How do you heat your home?

2. Do you have a gas stove or an electric stove?

3. What are some ways you can save energy when it's cold?

4. Do you recycle? What products do you recycle?

5. Does your market have recycling bins?

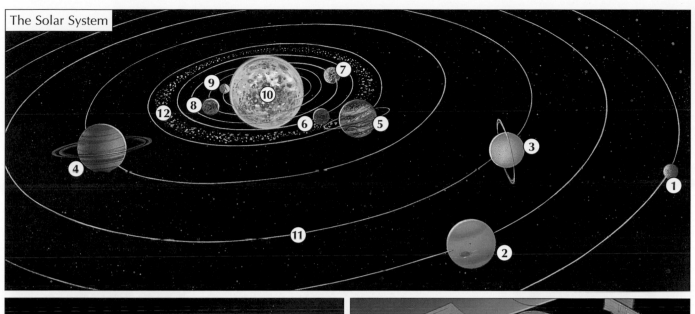

The Solar System

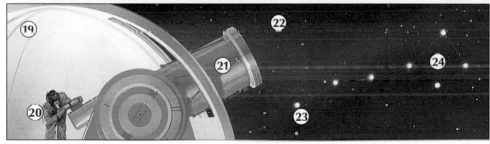

## The planets

**1.** Pluto

**2.** Neptune

**3.** Uranus

**4.** Saturn

**5.** Jupiter

**6.** Mars

**7.** Earth

**8.** Venus

**9.** Mercury

**10.** sun

**11.** orbit

**12.** asteroid belt

**13.** new moon

**14.** crescent moon

**15.** quarter moon

**16.** full moon

**17.** astronaut

**18.** space station

**19.** observatory

**20.** astronomer

**21.** telescope

**22.** space

**23.** star

**24.** constellation

**25.** comet

**26.** galaxy

## More vocabulary

**lunar eclipse:** when the earth is between the sun and the moon

**solar eclipse:** when the moon is between the earth and the sun

## Share your answers.

**1.** Do you know the names of any constellations?

**2.** How do you feel when you look up at the night sky?

**3.** Is the night sky in the U.S. the same as in your country?

# Trees and Plants

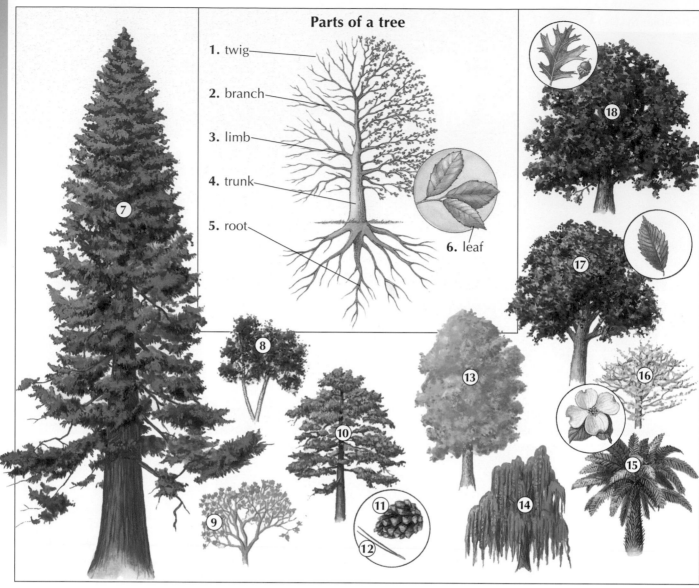

**Parts of a tree**

1. twig
2. branch
3. limb
4. trunk
5. root
6. leaf

| | | | |
|---|---|---|---|
| 7. redwood | 10. pine | 13. maple | 16. dogwood |
| 8. birch | 11. pinecone | 14. willow | 17. elm |
| 9. magnolia | 12. needle | 15. palm | 18. oak |

## Plants

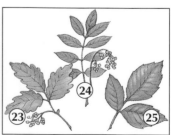

| | | | |
|---|---|---|---|
| 19. holly | 21. cactus | 23. poison oak | 25. poison ivy |
| 20. berries | 22. vine | 24. poison sumac | |

## Parts of a flower

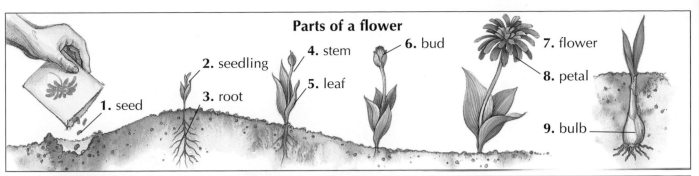

**1.** seed
**2.** seedling
**3.** root
**4.** stem
**5.** leaf
**6.** bud
**7.** flower
**8.** petal
**9.** bulb

**10.** sunflower

**11.** tulip

**12.** hibiscus

**13.** marigold

**14.** daisy

**15.** rose

**16.** gardenia

**17.** orchid

**18.** carnation

**19.** chrysanthemum

**20.** iris

**21.** jasmine

**22.** violet

**23.** poinsettia

**24.** lily

**25.** crocus

**26.** daffodil

**27.** bouquet

**28.** thorn

**29.** houseplant

# Marine Life, Amphibians, and Reptiles

## Parts of a fish

1. fin
2. gills
3. scales

## Sea animals

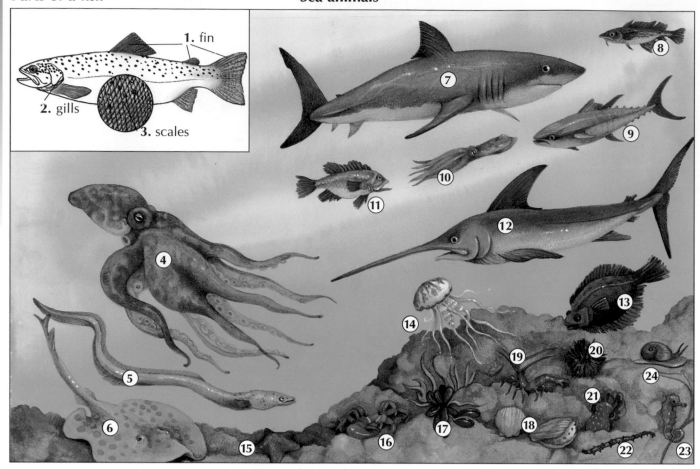

| | | |
|---|---|---|
| **4.** octopus | **11.** bass | **18.** scallop |
| **5.** eel | **12.** swordfish | **19.** shrimp |
| **6.** ray | **13.** flounder | **20.** sea urchin |
| **7.** shark | **14.** jellyfish | **21.** sea anemone |
| **8.** cod | **15.** starfish | **22.** worm |
| **9.** tuna | **16.** crab | **23.** sea horse |
| **10.** squid | **17.** mussel | **24.** snail |

## Amphibians

**25.** frog          **26.** newt          **27.** salamander          **28.** toad

130

## Sea mammals

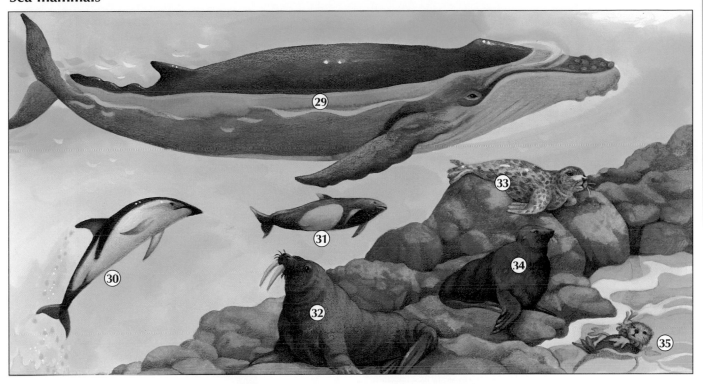

| | | | |
|---|---|---|---|
| **29.** whale | **31.** porpoise | **33.** seal | **35.** otter |
| **30.** dolphin | **32.** walrus | **34.** sea lion | |

## Reptiles

| | | | |
|---|---|---|---|
| **36.** alligator | **38.** rattlesnake | **40.** cobra | **42.** turtle |
| **37.** crocodile | **39.** garter snake | **41.** lizard | |

## Parts of a bird

1. beak / bill
2. wing
3. nest
4. claw
5. feather

| | | | |
|---|---|---|---|
| **6.** owl | **9.** woodpecker | **12.** penguin | **15.** peacock |
| **7.** blue jay | **10.** eagle | **13.** duck | **16.** pigeon |
| **8.** sparrow | **11.** hummingbird | **14.** goose | **17.** robin |

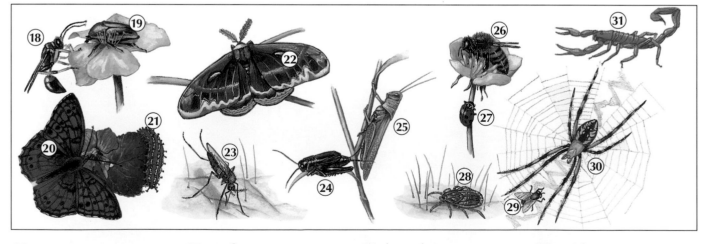

| | | | |
|---|---|---|---|
| **18.** wasp | **22.** moth | **26.** honeybee | **30.** spider |
| **19.** beetle | **23.** mosquito | **27.** ladybug | **31.** scorpion |
| **20.** butterfly | **24.** cricket | **28.** tick | |
| **21.** caterpillar | **25.** grasshopper | **29.** fly | |

## Farm animals

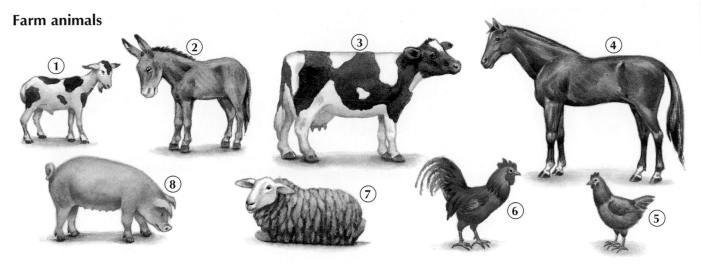

| | |
|---|---|
| **1.** goat | **3.** cow |
| **2.** donkey | **4.** horse |

| | |
|---|---|
| **5.** hen | **7.** sheep |
| **6.** rooster | **8.** pig |

## Pets

| | |
|---|---|
| **9.** cat | **11.** dog |
| **10.** kitten | **12.** puppy |

| | |
|---|---|
| **13.** rabbit | **15.** parakeet |
| **14.** guinea pig | **16.** goldfish |

## Rodents

| | | |
|---|---|---|
| **17.** mouse | **19.** gopher | **21.** squirrel |
| **18.** rat | **20.** chipmunk | **22.** prairie dog |

### More vocabulary

**Wild animals** live, eat, and raise their young away from people, in the forests, mountains, plains, etc.

**Domesticated animals** work for people or live with them.

### Share your answers.

1. Do you have any pets? any farm animals?

2. Which of these animals are in your neighborhood? Which are not?

1. moose
2. mountain lion
3. coyote
4. opossum

5. wolf
6. buffalo/bison
7. bat
8. armadillo

9. beaver
10. porcupine
11. bear
12. skunk

13. raccoon
14. deer
15. fox

16. antler
17. hoof

18. whiskers
19. coat/fur

20. paw
21. horn

22. tail
23. quill

| | | | |
|---|---|---|---|
| **24.** anteater | **30.** gorilla | **36.** lion | **42.** elephant |
| **25.** leopard | **31.** hyena | **37.** tiger | **43.** hippopotamus |
| **26.** llama | **32.** baboon | **38.** camel | **44.** kangaroo |
| **27.** monkey | **33.** giraffe | **39.** panther | **45.** koala |
| **28.** chimpanzee | **34.** zebra | **40.** orangutan | **46.** platypus |
| **29.** rhinoceros | **35.** antelope | **41.** panda | |

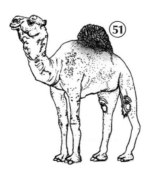

| | | | | |
|---|---|---|---|---|
| **47.** trunk | **48.** tusk | **49.** mane | **50.** pouch | **51.** hump |

# Jobs and Occupations, A–H

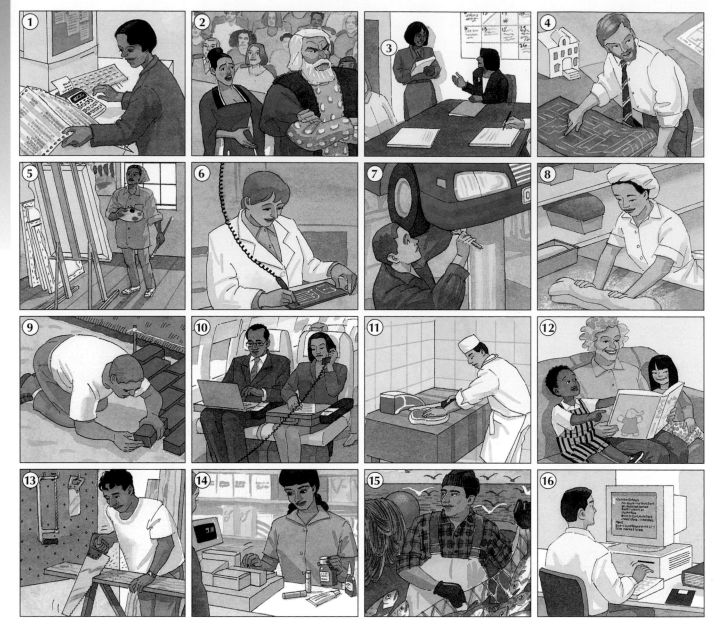

1. accountant
2. actor
3. administrative assistant
4. architect
5. artist
6. assembler

7. auto mechanic
8. baker
9. bricklayer
10. businessman/businesswoman
11. butcher
12. caregiver/baby-sitter

13. carpenter
14. cashier
15. commercial fisher
16. computer programmer

**Use the new language.**

1. Who works outside?
2. Who works inside?
3. Who makes things?

4. Who uses a computer?
5. Who wears a uniform?
6. Who sells things?

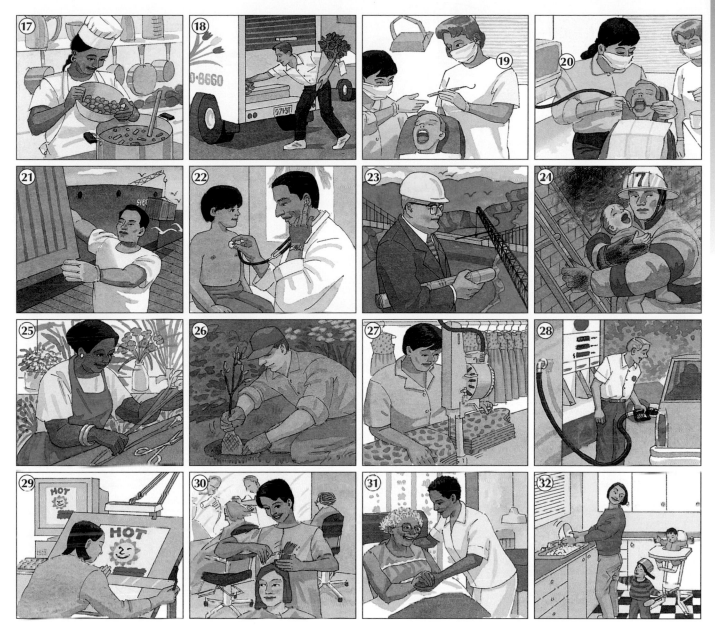

| | | |
|---|---|---|
| **17.** cook | **23.** engineer | **29.** graphic artist |
| **18.** delivery person | **24.** firefighter | **30.** hairdresser |
| **19.** dental assistant | **25.** florist | **31.** home attendant |
| **20.** dentist | **26.** gardener | **32.** homemaker |
| **21.** dockworker | **27.** garment worker | |
| **22.** doctor | **28.** gas station attendant | |

### Share your answers.

**1.** Do you know people who have some of these jobs? What do they say about their work?

**2.** Which of these jobs are available in your city?

**3.** For which of these jobs do you need special training?

| | | |
|---|---|---|
| **33.** housekeeper | **39.** model | **45.** postal worker |
| **34.** interpreter / translator | **40.** mover | **46.** printer |
| **35.** janitor / custodian | **41.** musician | **47.** receptionist |
| **36.** lawyer | **42.** nurse | **48.** repair person |
| **37.** machine operator | **43.** painter | |
| **38.** messenger / courier | **44.** police officer | |

**Talk about each of the jobs or occupations.**

*She's a housekeeper. She works in a hotel.*
*He's an interpreter. He works for the government.*

*She's a nurse. She works with patients.*

**49.** reporter

**50.** salesclerk/salesperson

**51.** sanitation worker

**52.** secretary

**53.** server

**54.** serviceman/servicewoman

**55.** stock clerk

**56.** store owner

**57.** student

**58.** teacher/instructor

**59.** telemarketer

**60.** travel agent

**61.** truck driver

**62.** veterinarian

**63.** welder

**64.** writer/author

**Talk about your job or the job you want.**

*What do you do?*

   *I'm a salesclerk. I work in a store.*

*What do you want to do?*

   *I want to be a veterinarian. I want to work with animals.*

# Job Skills

A. **assemble** components

B. **assist** medical patients

C. **cook**

D. **do** manual labor

E. **drive** a truck

F. **operate** heavy machinery

G. **repair** appliances

H. **sell** cars

I. **sew** clothes

J. **speak** another language

K. **supervise** people

L. **take care** of children

M. **type**

N. **use** a cash register

O. **wait on** customers

P. **work** on a computer

## More vocabulary

**act:** to perform in a play, movie, or TV show

**fly:** to pilot an airplane

**teach:** to instruct, to show how to do something

## Share your answers.

1. What job skills do you have? Where did you learn them?

2. What job skills do you want to learn?

**A. talk** to friends

**B. look** at a job board

**C. look** for a help wanted sign

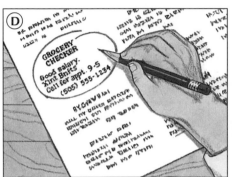

**D. look** in the classifieds

**E. call** for information

**F. ask** about the hours

**G. fill out** an application

**H. go** on an interview

**I. talk** about your experience

**J. ask** about benefits

**K. inquire** about the salary

**L. get hired**

# An Office

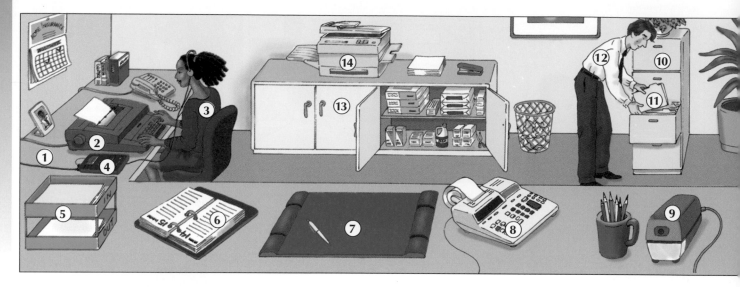

1. desk

2. typewriter

3. secretary

4. microcassette transcriber

5. stacking tray

6. desk calendar

7. desk pad

8. calculator

9. electric pencil sharpener

10. file cabinet

11. file folder

12. file clerk

13. supply cabinet

14. photocopier

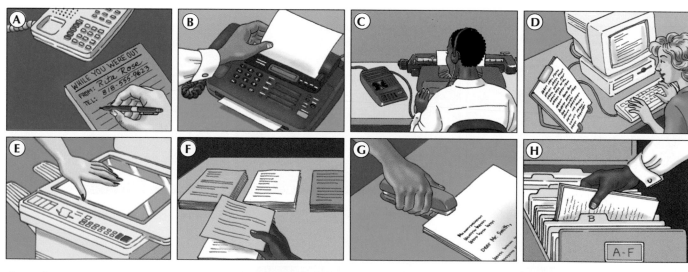

A. **take** a message

B. **fax** a letter

C. **transcribe** notes

D. **type** a letter

E. **make** copies

F. **collate** papers

G. **staple**

H. **file** papers

**Practice taking messages.**

*Hello. My name is <u>Sara Scott</u>. Is <u>Mr. Lee</u> in?*

*Not yet. Would you like to leave a message?*

*Yes. Please ask <u>him</u> to call me at <u>555-4859</u>.*

**Share your answers.**

1. Which office equipment do you know how to use?

2. Which jobs does a file clerk do?

3. Which jobs does a secretary do?

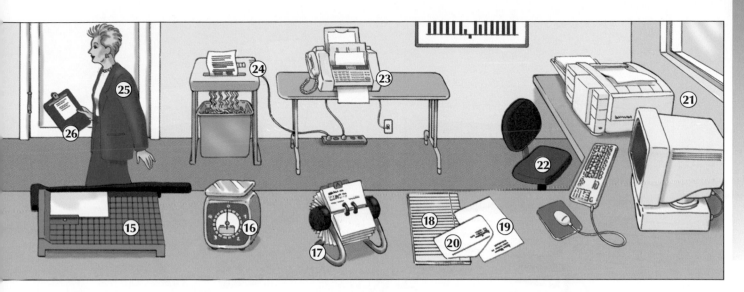

15. paper cutter

16. postal scale

17. rotary card file

18. legal pad

19. letterhead paper

20. envelope

21. computer workstation

22. swivel chair

23. fax machine

24. paper shredder

25. office manager

26. clipboard

27. appointment book

28. stapler

29. staple

30. organizer

31. typewriter cartridge

32. mailer

33. correction fluid

34. Post-it notes

35. label

36. notepad

37. glue

38. rubber cement

39. clear tape

40. rubber stamp

41. ink pad

42. packing tape

43. pushpin

44. paper clip

45. rubber band

**Use the new language.**

1. Which items keep things together?

2. Which items are used to mail packages?

3. Which items are made of paper?

**Share your answers.**

1. Which office supplies do students use?

2. Where can you buy them?

## Hardware

**1.** CPU (central processing unit)

**2.** CD-ROM disc

**3.** disk drive

**4.** power switch

**5.** disk/floppy

**6.** monitor/screen

**7.** keyboard

**8.** mouse

**9.** joystick

**10.** surge protector

**11.** modem

**12.** printer

**13.** scanner

**14.** laptop

**15.** trackball

**16.** cable

**17.** port

**18.** motherboard

**19.** slot

**20.** hard disk drive

## Software

**21.** program/application

**22.** user's manual

## More vocabulary

**data:** information that a computer can read

**memory:** how much data a computer can hold

**speed:** how fast a computer can work with data

## Share your answers.

**1.** Can you use a computer?

**2.** How did you learn? in school? from a book? by yourself?

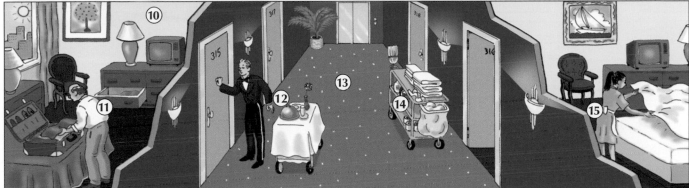

1. valet parking

2. doorman

3. lobby

4. bell captain

5. bellhop

6. luggage cart

7. gift shop

8. front desk

9. desk clerk

10. guest room

11. guest

12. room service

13. hall

14. housekeeping cart

15. housekeeper

16. pool

17. pool service

18. ice machine

19. meeting room

20. ballroom

**More vocabulary**

**concierge:** the hotel worker who helps guests find restaurants and interesting places to go

**service elevator:** an elevator for hotel workers

**Share your answers.**

1. Does this look like a hotel in your city? Which one?
2. Which hotel job is the most difficult?
3. How much does it cost to stay in a hotel in your city?

# A Factory

| | | |
|---|---|---|
| **1.** front office | **7.** parts | **13.** packer |
| **2.** factory owner | **8.** assembly line | **14.** forklift |
| **3.** designer | **9.** warehouse | **15.** shipping clerk |
| **4.** time clock | **10.** order puller | **16.** loading dock |
| **5.** line supervisor | **11.** hand truck | |
| **6.** factory worker | **12.** conveyor belt | |

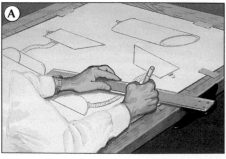

**A. design**

**B. manufacture**

**C. ship**

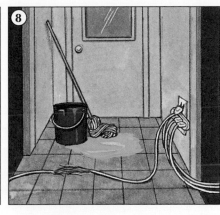

**1.** electrical hazard

**2.** flammable

**3.** poison

**4.** corrosive

**5.** biohazard

**6.** radioactive

**7.** hazardous materials

**8.** dangerous situation

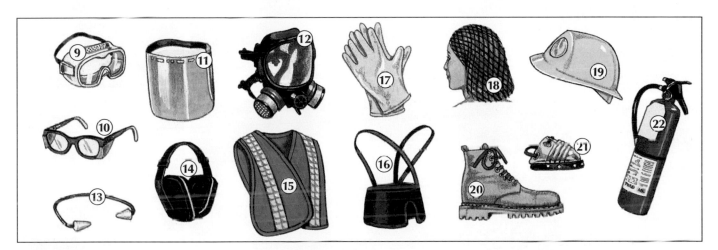

**9.** safety goggles

**10.** safety glasses

**11.** safety visor

**12.** respirator

**13.** earplugs

**14.** safety earmuffs

**15.** safety vest

**16.** back support

**17.** latex gloves

**18.** hair net

**19.** hard hat

**20.** safety boot

**21.** toe guard

**22.** fire extinguisher

**23.** careless

**24.** careful

# Farming and Ranching

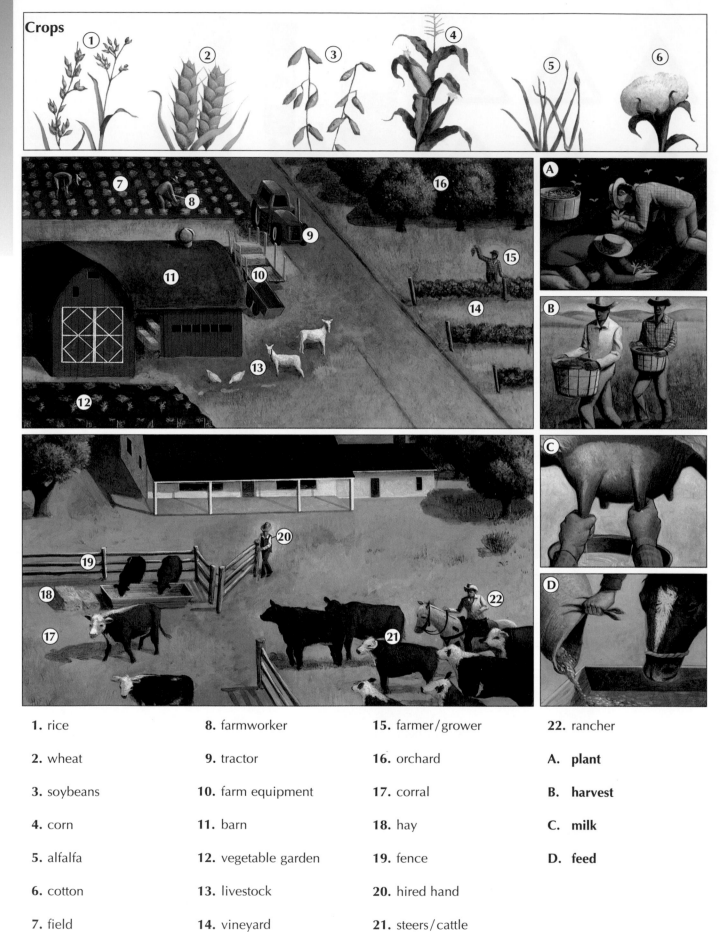

**Crops**

| | | |
|---|---|---|
| **1.** rice | **8.** farmworker | **15.** farmer/grower | **22.** rancher |
| **2.** wheat | **9.** tractor | **16.** orchard | **A. plant** |
| **3.** soybeans | **10.** farm equipment | **17.** corral | **B. harvest** |
| **4.** corn | **11.** barn | **18.** hay | **C. milk** |
| **5.** alfalfa | **12.** vegetable garden | **19.** fence | **D. feed** |
| **6.** cotton | **13.** livestock | **20.** hired hand | |
| **7.** field | **14.** vineyard | **21.** steers/cattle | |

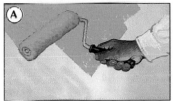

1. construction worker
2. ladder
3. I beam / girder
4. scaffolding
5. cherry picker
6. bulldozer
7. crane
8. backhoe
9. jackhammer / pneumatic drill

10. concrete
11. bricks
12. trowel
13. insulation
14. stucco
15. window pane
16. plywood
17. wood / lumber
18. drywall

19. shingles
20. pickax
21. shovel
22. sledgehammer

A. **paint**
B. **lay** bricks
C. **measure**
D. **hammer**

| | | | |
|---|---|---|---|
| **1.** hammer | **4.** handsaw | **7.** pliers | **10.** circular saw |
| **2.** mallet | **5.** hacksaw | **8.** electric drill | **11.** blade |
| **3.** ax | **6.** C-clamp | **9.** power sander | **12.** router |

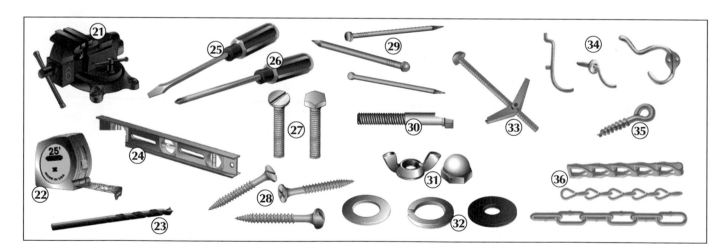

| | | | |
|---|---|---|---|
| **21.** vise | **25.** screwdriver | **29.** nail | **33.** toggle bolt |
| **22.** tape measure | **26.** Phillips screwdriver | **30.** bolt | **34.** hook |
| **23.** drill bit | **27.** machine screw | **31.** nut | **35.** eye hook |
| **24.** level | **28.** wood screw | **32.** washer | **36.** chain |

**Use the new language.**

1. Which tools are used for plumbing?

2. Which tools are used for painting?

3. Which tools are used for electrical work?

4. Which tools are used for working with wood?

**13.** wire

**14.** extension cord

**15.** yardstick

**16.** pipe

**17.** fittings

**18.** wood

**19.** spray gun

**20.** paint

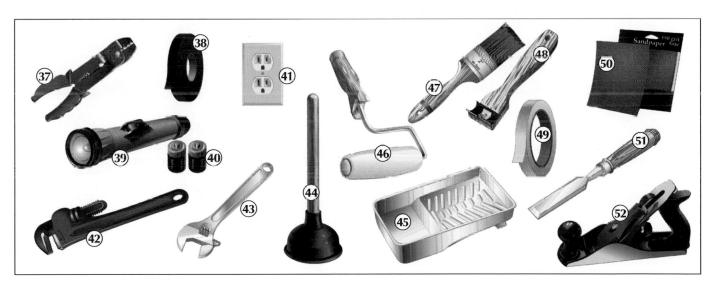

**37.** wire stripper

**38.** electrical tape

**39.** flashlight

**40.** battery

**41.** outlet

**42.** pipe wrench

**43.** wrench

**44.** plunger

**45.** paint pan

**46.** paint roller

**47.** paintbrush

**48.** scraper

**49.** masking tape

**50.** sandpaper

**51.** chisel

**52.** plane

**Use the new language.**

Look at **Household Problems and Repairs,**
pages **48–49.**

Name the tools you use to fix the problems you see.

**Share your answers.**

1. Which tools do you have in your home?

2. Which tools can be dangerous to use?

# Places to Go

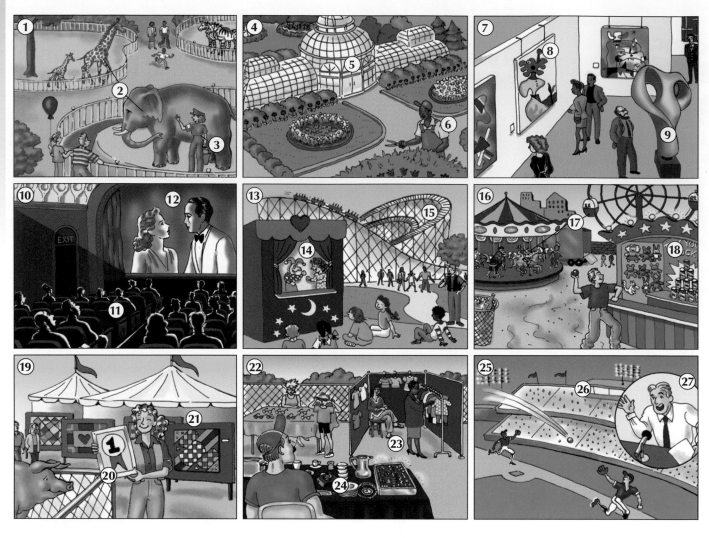

1. zoo

2. animals

3. zookeeper

4. botanical gardens

5. greenhouse

6. gardener

7. art museum

8. painting

9. sculpture

10. the movies

11. seat

12. screen

13. amusement park

14. puppet show

15. roller coaster

16. carnival

17. rides

18. game

19. county fair

20. first place/first prize

21. exhibition

22. swap meet/flea market

23. booth

24. merchandise

25. baseball game

26. stadium

27. announcer

**Talk about the places you like to go.**

*I like <u>animals</u>, so I go to <u>the zoo</u>.*

*I like <u>rides</u>, so I go to <u>carnivals</u>.*

**Share your answers.**

1. Which of these places is interesting to you?

2. Which rides do you like at an amusement park?

3. What are some famous places to go to in your country?

1. ball field

2. bike path

3. cyclist

4. bicycle/bike

5. jump rope

6. duck pond

7. tennis court

8. picnic table

9. tricycle

10. bench

11. water fountain

12. swings

13. slide

14. climbing apparatus

15. sandbox

16. seesaw

A. **pull** the wagon

B. **push** the swing

C. **climb** on the bars

D. **picnic/have** a picnic

| | | |
|---|---|---|
| **1.** camping | **4.** rafting | **7.** backpacking |
| **2.** boating | **5.** fishing | **8.** mountain biking |
| **3.** canoeing | **6.** hiking | **9.** horseback riding |

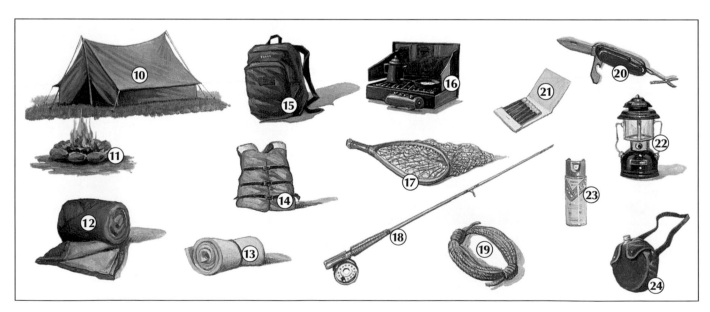

| | | |
|---|---|---|
| **10.** tent | **15.** backpack | **20.** multi-use knife |
| **11.** campfire | **16.** camping stove | **21.** matches |
| **12.** sleeping bag | **17.** fishing net | **22.** lantern |
| **13.** foam pad | **18.** fishing pole | **23.** insect repellent |
| **14.** life vest | **19.** rope | **24.** canteen |

1. ocean/water

2. fins

3. diving mask

4. sailboat

5. surfboard

6. wave

7. wet suit

8. scuba tank

9. beach umbrella

10. sand castle

11. cooler

12. shade

13. sunscreen/sunblock

14. beach chair

15. beach towel

16. pier

17. sunbather

18. lifeguard

19. lifesaving device

20. lifeguard station

21. seashell

22. pail/bucket

23. sand

24. rock

**More vocabulary**

**seaweed:** a plant that grows in the ocean

**tide:** the level of the ocean. The tide goes in and out every twelve hours.

**Share your answers.**

1. Are there any beaches near your home?

2. Do you prefer to spend more time on the sand or in the water?

3. Where are some of the world's best beaches?

A. walk

B. jog

C. run

D. throw

E. catch

F. pitch

G. hit

H. pass

I. shoot

J. jump

K. dribble / bounce

L. kick

M. tackle

**Practice talking about what you can do.**

*I can swim, but I can't dive.*

*I can pass the ball well, but I can't shoot too well.*

**Use the new language.**

Look at **Individual Sports,** page **159.**

Name the actions you see people doing.

*The man in number 18 is riding a horse.*

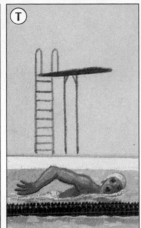

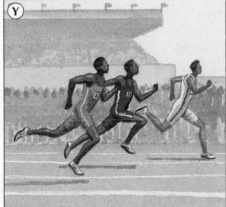

FINISH

| N. serve | R. bend | V. skate | Z. finish |
| O. swing | S. dive | W. ride | |
| P. exercise / work out | T. swim | X. start | |
| Q. stretch | U. ski | Y. race | |

**Share your answers.**

1. What do you like to do?
2. What do you have difficulty doing?
3. How often do you exercise? Once a week? Two or three times a week? More? Never?
4. Which is more difficult, throwing a ball or catching it?

1. score
2. coach
3. team
4. fan
5. player
6. official/referee
7. basketball court

8. basketball
9. baseball
10. softball
11. football
12. soccer
13. ice hockey
14. volleyball
15. water polo

**More vocabulary**

**captain:** the team leader

**umpire:** in baseball, the name for the referee

**Little League:** a baseball league for children

**win:** to have the best score

**lose:** the opposite of win

**tie:** to have the same score as the other team

1. archery
2. billiards/pool
3. bowling
4. cycling/biking
5. fencing

6. flying disc*
7. golf
8. gymnastics
9. inline skating
10. martial arts

11. racquetball
12. skateboarding
13. table tennis/ Ping-Pong™
14. tennis
15. weightlifting

16. wrestling
17. track and field
18. horse racing

*Note: one brand is Frisbee® (Mattel, Inc.)

## Talk about sports.

*Which sports do you like?*

   *I like tennis but I don't like golf.*

## Share your answers.

1. Which sports are good for children to learn? Why?
2. Which sport is the most difficult to learn? Why?
3. Which sport is the most dangerous? Why?

1. downhill skiing

2. snowboarding

3. cross-country skiing

4. ice skating

5. figure skating

6. sledding

7. waterskiing

8. sailing

9. surfing

10. sailboarding

11. snorkeling

12. scuba diving

**Use the new language.**

Look at **The Beach,** page **155.**

Name the sports you see.

**Share your answers.**

1. Which sports are in the Winter Olympics?

2. Which sports do you think are the most exciting to watch?

1. golf club

2. tennis racket

3. volleyball

4. basketball

5. bowling ball

6. bow

7. arrow

8. target

9. ice skates

10. inline skates

11. hockey stick

12. soccer ball

13. shin guards

14. baseball bat

15. catcher's mask

16. uniform

17. glove

18. baseball

19. weights

20. football helmet

21. shoulder pads

22. football

23. snowboard

24. skis

25. ski poles

26. ski boots

27. flying disc*

*Note: one brand is Frisbee®
(Mattel, Inc.)

**Share your answers.**

1. Which sports equipment is used for safety reasons?

2. Which sports equipment is heavy?

3. What sports equipment do you have at home?

**Use the new language.**

Look at **Individual Sports,** page **159.**

Name the sports equipment you see.

| A. **collect** things | B. **play** games | C. **build** models | D. **do** crafts |

| 1. video game system | 5. checkers | 9. acrylic paint | 13. coin collection |
| 2. cartridge | 6. chess | 10. figurine | 14. clay |
| 3. board game | 7. model kit | 11. baseball card | 15. doll making kit |
| 4. dice | 8. glue | 12. stamp collection | 16. woodworking kit |

**Talk about how much time you spend on your hobbies.**

I _do crafts_ all the time.
I _play chess_ sometimes.
I never _build models_.

**Share your answers.**

1. How often do you play video games? Often? Sometimes? Never?
2. What board games do you know?
3. Do you collect anything? What?

**E.** **paint**  **F.** **knit**  **G.** **pretend**  **H.** **play** cards

**17.** yarn

**18.** knitting needles

**19.** embroidery

**20.** crochet

**21.** easel

**22.** canvas

**23.** paintbrush

**24.** oil paint

**25.** watercolor

**26.** clubs

**27.** diamonds

**28.** spades

**29.** hearts

**30.** paper doll

**31.** action figure

**32.** model trains

---

**Share your answers.**

**1.** Do you like to play cards? Which games?

**2.** Did you pretend a lot when you were a child? What did you pretend to be?

**3.** Is it important to have hobbies? Why or why not?

**4.** What's your favorite game?

**5.** What's your hobby?

# Electronics and Photography

1. clock radio

2. portable radio-cassette player

3. cassette recorder

4. microphone

5. shortwave radio

6. TV (television)

7. portable TV

8. VCR (videocassette recorder)

9. remote control

10. videocassette

11. speakers

12. turntable

13. tuner

14. CD player

15. personal radio-cassette player

16. headphones

17. adapter

18. plug

19. video camera

20. tripod

21. camcorder

22. battery pack

23. battery charger

24. 35 mm camera

25. zoom lens

26. film

27. camera case

28. screen

29. carousel slide projector

30. slide tray

31. slides

32. photo album

33. out of focus

34. overexposed

35. underexposed

A. **record**

B. **play**

C. **fast forward**

D. **rewind**

E. **pause**

F. **stop** and **eject**

# Entertainment

## Types of entertainment

**1.** film/movie

**2.** play

**3.** television program

**4.** radio program

**5.** stand-up comedy

**6.** concert

**7.** ballet

**8.** opera

## Types of stories

**9.** western

**10.** comedy

**11.** tragedy

**12.** science fiction story

**13.** action story/ adventure story

**14.** horror story

**15.** mystery

**16.** romance

## Types of TV programs

**17.** news

**18.** sitcom (situation comedy)

**19.** cartoon

**20.** talk show

**21.** soap opera

**22.** nature program

**23.** game show/quiz show

**24.** children's program

**25.** shopping program

**26. serious** book

**27. funny** book

**28. sad** book

**29. boring** book

**30. interesting** book

# Holidays

1. New Year's Day

2. parade

3. confetti

4. Valentine's Day

5. card

6. heart

7. Independence Day/4th of July

8. fireworks

9. flag

10. Halloween

11. jack-o'-lantern

12. mask

13. costume

14. candy

15. Thanksgiving

16. feast

17. turkey

18. Christmas

19. ornament

20. Christmas tree

**A. plan** a party

**B. invite** the guests

**C. decorate** the house

**D. wrap** a gift

**E. hide**

**F. answer** the door

**G. shout** "surprise!"

**H. light** the candles

**I. sing** "Happy Birthday"

**J. make** a wish

**K. blow out** the candles

**L. open** the presents

---

**Practice inviting friends to a party.**

*I'd love for you to come to my party <u>next week</u>.*

*Could <u>you and your friend</u> come to my party?*

*Would <u>your friend</u> like to come to a party I'm giving?*

**Share your answers.**

**1.** Do you celebrate birthdays? What do you do?

**2.** Are there birthdays you celebrate in a special way?

**3.** Is there a special birthday song in your country?

# Verb Guide

Verbs in English are either regular or irregular in the past tense and past participle forms.

**Regular Verbs**

The regular verbs below are marked 1, 2, 3, or 4 according to four different spelling patterns. (See page 172 for the **irregular verbs** which do not follow any of these patterns.)

| *Spelling Patterns for the Past and the Past Participle* | *Example* | | |
|---|---|---|---|
| **1.** Add **-ed** to the end of the verb. | **ASK** | → | **ASKED** |
| **2.** Add **-d** to the end of the verb. | **LIVE** | → | **LIVED** |
| **3.** Double the final consonant and add **-ed** to the end of the verb. | **DROP** | → | **DROPPED** |
| **4.** Drop the final y and add **-ied** to the end of the verb. | **CRY** | → | **CRIED** |

## The Oxford Picture Dictionary List of Regular Verbs

act (1)
add (1)
address (1)
answer (1)
apologize (2)
appear (1)
applaud (1)
arrange (2)
arrest (1)
arrive (2)
ask (1)
assemble (2)
assist (1)
bake (2)
barbecue (2)
bathe (2)
board (1)
boil (1)
borrow (1)
bounce (2)
brainstorm (1)
breathe (2)
broil (1)
brush (1)
burn (1)
call (1)
carry (4)
change (2)
check (1)
choke (2)
chop (3)
circle (2)
claim (1)
clap (3)
clean (1)
clear (1)
climb (1)
close (2)
collate (2)

collect (1)
color (1)
comb (1)
commit (3)
compliment (1)
conserve (2)
convert (1)
cook (1)
copy (4)
correct (1)
cough (1)
count (1)
cross (1)
cry (4)
dance (2)
design (1)
deposit (1)
deliver (1)
dial (1)
dictate (2)
die (2)
discuss (1)
dive (2)
dress (1)
dribble (2)
drill (1)
drop (3)
drown (1)
dry (4)
dust (1)
dye (2)
edit (1)
eject (1)
empty (4)
end (1)
enter (1)
erase (2)
examine (2)
exchange (2)

exercise (2)
experience (2)
exterminate (2)
fasten (1)
fax (1)
file (2)
fill (1)
finish (1)
fix (1)
floss (1)
fold (1)
fry (4)
gargle (2)
graduate (2)
grate (2)
grease (2)
greet (1)
grill (1)
hail (1)
hammer (1)
harvest (1)
help (1)
hire (2)
hug (3)
immigrate (2)
inquire (2)
insert (1)
introduce (2)
invite (2)
iron (1)
jog (3)
join (1)
jump (1)
kick (1)
kiss (1)
knit (3)
land (1)
laugh (1)
learn (1)

| | | |
|---|---|---|
| lengthen (1) | pull (1) | start (1) |
| listen (1) | push (1) | stay (1) |
| live (2) | race (2) | steam (1) |
| load (1) | raise (2) | stir (3) |
| lock (1) | rake (2) | stir-fry (4) |
| look (1) | receive (2) | stop (3) |
| mail (1) | record (1) | stow (1) |
| manufacture (2) | recycle (2) | stretch (1) |
| mark (1) | register (1) | supervise (2) |
| match (1) | relax (1) | swallow (1) |
| measure (2) | remove (2) | tackle (2) |
| milk (1) | rent (1) | talk (1) |
| miss (1) | repair (1) | taste (2) |
| mix (1) | repeat (1) | thank (1) |
| mop (3) | report (1) | tie (2) |
| move (2) | request (1) | touch (1) |
| mow (1) | return (1) | transcribe (2) |
| need (1) | rinse (2) | transfer (3) |
| nurse (2) | roast (1) | travel (1) |
| obey (1) | rock (1) | trim (3) |
| observe (2) | sauté (2) | turn (1) |
| open (1) | save (2) | type (2) |
| operate (2) | scrub (3) | underline (2) |
| order (1) | seat (1) | unload (1) |
| overdose (2) | sentence (2) | unpack (1) |
| paint (1) | serve (2) | use (2) |
| park (1) | share (2) | vacuum (1) |
| pass (1) | shave (2) | vomit (1) |
| pause (2) | ship (3) | vote (2) |
| peel (1) | shop (3) | wait (1) |
| perm (1) | shorten (1) | walk (1) |
| pick (1) | shout (1) | wash (1) |
| pitch (1) | sign (1) | watch (1) |
| plan (3) | simmer (1) | water (1) |
| plant (1) | skate (2) | weed (1) |
| play (1) | ski (1) | weigh (1) |
| point (1) | slice (2) | wipe (2) |
| polish (1) | smell (1) | work (1) |
| pour (1) | sneeze (2) | wrap (3) |
| pretend (1) | sort (1) | yield (1) |
| print (1) | spell (1) | |
| protect (1) | staple (2) | |

# Verb Guide

## Irregular Verbs

These verbs have irregular endings in the past and/or the past participle.

### The Oxford Picture Dictionary List of Irregular Verbs

| simple | past | past participle | simple | past | past participle |
|--------|------|-----------------|--------|------|-----------------|
| be | was | been | leave | left | left |
| beat | beat | beaten | lend | lent | lent |
| become | became | become | let | let | let |
| begin | began | begun | light | lit | lit |
| bend | bent | bent | make | made | made |
| bleed | bled | bled | pay | paid | paid |
| blow | blew | blown | picnic | picnicked | picnicked |
| break | broke | broken | put | put | put |
| build | built | built | read | read | read |
| buy | bought | bought | rewind | rewound | rewound |
| catch | caught | caught | rewrite | rewrote | rewritten |
| come | came | come | ride | rode | ridden |
| cut | cut | cut | run | ran | run |
| do | did | done | say | said | said |
| draw | drew | drawn | see | saw | seen |
| drink | drank | drunk | sell | sold | sold |
| drive | drove | driven | send | sent | sent |
| eat | ate | eaten | set | set | set |
| fall | fell | fallen | sew | sewed | sewn |
| feed | fed | fed | shoot | shot | shot |
| feel | felt | felt | sing | sang | sung |
| find | found | found | sit | sat | sat |
| fly | flew | flown | speak | spoke | spoken |
| get | got | gotten | stand | stood | stood |
| give | gave | given | sweep | swept | swept |
| go | went | gone | swim | swam | swum |
| hang | hung | hung | swing | swung | swung |
| have | had | had | take | took | taken |
| hear | heard | heard | teach | taught | taught |
| hide | hid | hidden | throw | threw | thrown |
| hit | hit | hit | wake | woke | woken |
| hold | held | held | wear | wore | worn |
| keep | kept | kept | withdraw | withdrew | withdrawn |
| lay | laid | laid | write | wrote | written |

# Index

Two numbers are shown after words in the index: the first refers to the page where the word is illustrated and the second refers to the item number of the word on that page. For example, cool [ko͞ol] **10**-3 means that the word *cool* is item number 3 on page 10. If only the bold page number appears, then that word is part of the unit title or subtitle, or is found somewhere else on the page. A bold number followed by ✦ means the word can be found in the exercise space at the bottom of that page.

Words or combinations of words that appear in **bold** type are used as verbs or verb phrases. Words used as other parts of speech are shown in ordinary type. So, for example, **file** (in bold type) is the verb *file*, while file (in ordinary type) is the noun *file*. Words or phrases in small capital letters (for example, HOLIDAYS) form unit titles.

Phrases and other words that form combinations with an individual word entry are often listed underneath it. Rather than repeating the word each time it occurs in combination with what is listed under it, the word is replaced by three dots (...), called an ellipsis. For example, under the word *bus*, you will find ...driver and ...stop meaning *bus driver* and *bus stop*. Under the word *store* you will find shoe... and toy..., meaning *shoe store* and *toy store*.

## Pronunciation Guide

The index includes a pronunciation guide for all the words and phrases illustrated in the book. This guide uses symbols commonly found in dictionaries for native speakers. These symbols, unlike those used in pronunciation systems such as the International Phonetic Alphabet, tend to use English spelling patterns and so should help you to become more aware of the connections between written English and spoken English.

### Consonants

| | | |
|---|---|---|
| [b] as in back [băk] | [k] as in key [kē] | [sh] as in shoe [sho͞o] |
| [ch] as in cheek [chēk] | [l] as in leaf [lēf] | [t] as in tape [tāp] |
| [d] as in date [dāt] | [m] as in match [măch] | [th] as in three [thrē] |
| [dh] as in this [dhĭs] | [n] as in neck [nĕk] | [v] as in vine [vīn] |
| [f] as in face [fās] | [ng] as in ring [rĭng] | [w] as in wait [wāt] |
| [g] as in gas [găs] | [p] as in park [pärk] | [y] as in yams [yămz] |
| [h] as in half [hăf] | [r] as in rice [rīs] | [z] as in zoo [zo͞o] |
| [j] as in jam [jăm] | [s] as in sand [sănd] | [zh] as in measure [mĕzh/ər] |

### Vowels

| | | |
|---|---|---|
| [ā] as in bake [bāk] | [ĭ] as in lip [lĭp] | [ow] as in cow [kow] |
| [ă] as in back [băk] | [ï] as in near [nïr] | [oy] as in boy [boy] |
| [ä] as in car [kär] or box [bäks] | [ō] as in cold [kōld] | [ŭ] as in cut [kŭt] |
| [e] as in beat [bēt] | [ö] as in short [shört] | [ü] as in curb [kürb] |
| [ĕ] as in bed [bĕd] | or claw [klö] | [ə] as in above [ə bŭv/] |
| [ë] as in hear [bër] | [o͞o] as in cool [ko͞ol] | |
| [ī] as in line [līn] | [o͝o] as in cook [ko͝ok] | |

All the pronunciation symbols used are alphabetical except for the schwa [ə]. The schwa is the most frequent vowel sound in English. If you use the schwa appropriately in unstressed syllables, your pronunciation will sound more natural.

Vowels before [r] are shown with the symbol [¨] to call attention to the special quality that vowels have before [r] (Note that the symbols [ä] and [ö] are also used for vowels not followed by [r], as in *box* or *claw*.) You should listen carefully to native speakers to discover how these vowels actually sound.

### Stress

This index follows the system for marking stress used in many dictionaries for native speakers.

**1.** Stress is not marked if a word consisting of a single syllable occurs by itself.

**2.** Where stress is marked, two levels are distinguished:

a bold accent [/] is placed after each syllable with primary (or strong) stress, a light accent [/] is placed after each syllable with secondary (or weaker) stress.

In phrases and other combinations of words, stress is indicated for each word as it would be pronounced within the whole phrase or other unit. If a word consisting of a single syllable is stressed in the combinations listed below it, the accent mark indicating the degree of stress it has in the phrases (primary or secondary) is shown in parentheses. A hyphen replaces any part of a word or phrase that is omitted. For example, bus [bŭs(/–)] shows that the word *bus* is said with primary stress in the combinations shown below it. The word ...driver [–drī/vər], listed under *bus*, shows that *driver* has secondary stress in the combination *bus driver*: [bŭs/ drī/vər]

### Syllable Boundaries

Syllable boundaries are indicated by a single space or by a stress mark.

**Note:** The pronunciations shown in this index are based on patterns of American English. There has been no attempt to represent all of the varieties of American English. Students should listen to native speakers to hear how the language actually sounds in a particular region.

# Index

# Index

# Index

# Index

# Index

# Index

# Index

# Index

# Index

# Index

# Index

# Index

# Index

# Index

# Index

# Geographical Index

## Continents

## Countries and other locations